OUTPERFORM THE DOW

Wiley Trading Advantage Series

OUTPERFORM THE DOW

Using Options, Futures, and Portfolio Strategies to Beat the Market

GUNTER MEISSNER
&
RANDALL FOLSOM

JOHN WILEY & SONS, INC.

New York • Chichester • Weinheim • Brisbane • Singapore • Toronto

This book is printed on acid-free paper. ∞

Copyright © 2000 by Gunter Meissner. All rights reserved.

Published by John Wiley & Sons, Inc.

Published simultaneously in Canada.

No part of this publication may be reproduced, stored in a retrieval system or
transmitted in any form or by any means, electronic, mechanical, photocopying,
recording, scanning or otherwise, except as permitted under Sections 107 or 108 of
the 1976 United States Copyright Act, without either the prior written permission of
the Publisher, or authorization through payment of the appropriate per-copy fee to the
Copyright Clearance Center, 222 Rosewood Drive, Danvers, MA 01923, (978) 750-8400,
fax (978) 750-4744. Requests to the Publisher for permission should be addressed to
the Permissions Department, John Wiley & Sons, Inc., 605 Third Avenue, New York,
NY 10158-0012, (212) 850-6011, fax (212) 850-6008, E-Mail: PERMREQ @
WILEY.COM.

This publication is designed to provide accurate and authoritative information in
regard to the subject matter covered. It is sold with the understanding that the
publisher is not engaged in rendering professional services. If professional advice or
other expert assistance is required, the services of a competent professional person
should be sought.

Library of Congress Cataloging-in-Publication Data:
Meissner, Gunter, 1957–
    Outperform the Dow : using options, futures and portfolio strategies
to beat the market / Gunter Meissner, Randall Folsom.
       p. cm.—(Wiley trading advantage)
    Includes bibliographical references and index.
    ISBN 0-471-39311-8 (cloth : alk. paper)
    1. Dow Jones industrial average. 2. Stocks—Prices. 3. Options (Finance)
4. Futures. 5. Portfolio management. I. Folsom, Randall. II. Title. III. Series.

HG4915.M54 2000
332.64′—dc21   00-038134

Printed in the United States of America

10 9 8 7 6 5 4 3 2 1

To my parents, without whom I wouldn't be where I am.
Gunter Meissner

*To my wife Naomi and my daughter Emi for their support,
patience, and unconditional love.*
Randy Folsom

CONTENTS

ACKNOWLEDGMENTS

The authors would like to thank their research assistant Bogdan Zdziech, who supplied valuable ideas and did most of the calculations to derive the empirical results in this book. Our students Hans Clark, Johann Sandblohm, Vanessa Schlegel, Shigeharu Takemura, and Nicola Whistler proofread the book and contributed with helpful comments and suggestions.

PREFACE

This book is about money. Lots of money. And we care. Not only because we have Japanese wives and they are somewhat demanding, but because we believe that in our time it is important to know about investing and modern financial instruments. Being knowledgeable about finance makes life easier. It raises the efficiency of your work, makes it easier to put your kids through college, promises vacations in Hawaii, and most importantly, it ensures a secure retirement. All this can be achieved with a very low degree of risk.

The purpose of this book is to explain the Dow Jones Industrial Average and modern financial instruments to the reader. Using these new financial instruments we will derive investment strategies that exploit the seasonal and fundamental patterns of the Dow and individual companies. We will show that it is possible to systematically produce better returns than the Dow.

In Chapter 1, the history, composition and calculation of the Dow is explained. In Chapter 2 we show the contemporary methods to forecast stock prices and evaluate them. Chapter 3 deals with portfolio strategies concentrating on outperforming the Dow *and* minimizing risk. Chapter 4 explains futures and derives methods for beating the Dow with futures. Chapter 5 clarifies standard options and shows ways to outperform the Dow with standard options. In Chapter 6, the reoccurring volatility cycles of the Dow are exploited to derive maximum return strategies. In Chapter 7, exotic options are introduced and their practical application to maximize profits is explained.

1

THE DOW JONES INDUSTRIAL AVERAGE (DOW): HISTORY, COMPOSITION, CALCULATION

The greatest mistake made by the public is paying attention to prices, not values.

—Charles H. Dow

HISTORY OF THE DOW

In 1884, Charles H. Dow came up with the first list of eleven actively traded stocks, nine of which were railroads, and published them in the "Customer's Afternoon Letter," a forerunner to the *Wall Street Journal*. Dow's list went through several changes until his fledgling Dow Jones & Company came out with the first real version of the industrial index in May of 1886, a twelve stock average that at the time was still dominated by ten railroads. Over the next three months, the average promptly lost a quarter of its value, dipping to an all-time low of 28.48.

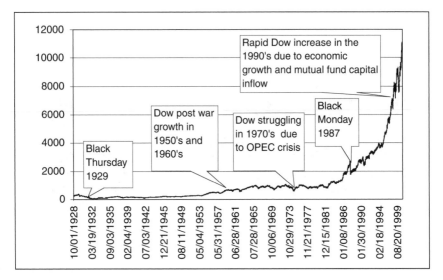

Figure 1.1   The Dow from 1928 to 1999

Since then, the Dow Jones Industrial Average, DJIA, (in this book, just "the Dow") has had a remarkable career. Figure 1.1 shows the development of the Dow from 1928 to 1999.

In the "Roaring Twenties," economies all over the world were expanding rapidly. Salaries were rising, consumer spending was high, and for the first time, investors heavily invested in the stock market. Many speculators invested their life savings, mortgaged their homes, and took credits to participate in the stock market. Because there had never been a stock market crash, caution was low and expectations were exuberant.

In the late stages of the bull market in 1929, some financial analysts predicted a coming correction, but their warnings were largely unheard in the midst of the buying frenzy. Finally, on Thursday, October 24, 1929, prices dwindled, investors began to sell, which turned into a wild selling frenzy. By the end of the day, the Dow had dropped by 12.9%.

In the following trading days, the selling panic continued and the Dow dropped further, losing 34% until the end of 1929. During the fall of the Dow it was not only financial institutions that lost millions of dollars. Many small investors had also speculated with their life savings and were financially ruined. Consequently, the "Great Depression" set in, resulting in millions of unemployed people and in hunger, thousands of bankruptcies, and economies shrinking worldwide.

After 1929, the Dow kept on sliding and reached its bottom in June 1932, having lost 86.2% of its value. It took the Dow until November 1954 to recover to the 380-point level it had attained in 1929.

After a sideways market during World War II, economic prosperity picked up in the 1950s and 1960s. The Dow reached 985 points in December 1968, but then a modest recession set in and it took the Dow until November 1972 to finally break the 1,000-point resistance.

The Dow was struggling in the 1970s and early 1980s. In 1973 and 1979 the OPEC (a cartel of oil exporting countries) raised oil prices drastically, which led to a recession in the western world. The Dow was still at 1,000 in October of 1982.

In the early 1980s, "Reaganomics," the supply-side supporting economic program of Ronald Reagan, fostered an incredible bull market. The Dow broke the 2,000-point barrier in January 1987. However, the bull market of the 1980s was interrupted by "Black Monday" on October 19, 1987, when the Dow suffered its biggest one-day drop in history of 508 points, or 22.6%. However, unlike Black Thursday of 1929, the market didn't suffer further significant declines. By the end of 1987, the Dow had already regained 11.5% of the October 19 loss. By August 1989, the Dow had fully recovered.

Stock market awareness has increased steadily in the 1990s. At the beginning of the decade, about 21% of American households owned stocks, by 1997, 43% of American households held stocks, often purchased cheaply and conveniently over the Internet.

With the steady economic growth in the 1990s, the Dow underwent a remarkable rally. In August 1991, the Dow broke the 3,000-point barrier, and in November 1995, the 5,000 barrier. Only three years later in March 1999, the Dow had doubled and broke the 10,000-point resistance.

As shown in Figure 1.1, we can conclude that investing in the Dow is a good idea. $100,000 invested in October 1982, when the Dow was at 1000, turned into $1,000,000 on March 29, 1999, when the Dow broke the 10,000-point barrier.

Looking at the Dow from a long-term cyclical perspective, one can find distinct bull and bear market periods (see Figure 1.2).

As seen in Figure 1.2, the first bear cycle started after the Black Monday in October 1929. The bear market was prolonged due to World War II until January 1950, when the Dow broke the 200-point barrier.

From 1950 until December 1968, post-World War II growth allowed an 18-year bull market. A mild recession started in 1968, and in 1973 and 1979 the two OPEC oil price increases led to a 14-year bear market that ended in August 1982.

Since 1982 the Dow has been enjoying a strong bull market. Naturally, the question arises: How long can this bull market continue? The previous bull market lasted 18 years, from 1950 to 1968.

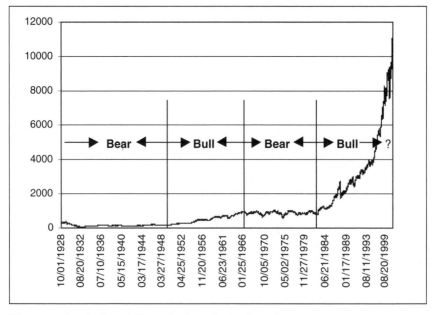

Figure 1.2   Bull and Bear Cycles of the Dow from 1928 to 1999

No bear or bull cycle since 1928 has lasted longer than 21 years. Does this suggest that the next bear market will begin in 2003, 21 years after the start of the bull market in 1982?

While the authors of this book do believe in the significance of repetitive long-term cycles, it is also evident that the length of several cycles was determined by exogenous events such as World War II and the OPEC oil price increases. Nevertheless, bull markets don't last forever. The historical maximum 21-year cycle should be kept in mind when bearish events, (e.g., a recession), occur at the beginning of the millennium. These bearish events can be underpinned by the historical long-term cyclical pattern.

Has the Dow Increased Too Far Too Fast?

The astonishing rally of the Dow, especially in the 1980s and 1990s, has raised concerns that the increase in the Dow has been too fast, and that a decrease is inevitable. However, Figures 1.1 and 1.2 show the *absolute* increase of the Dow. In *relative* or *percentage* terms, the increase has been fairly constant over the last 70 years, as shown in Figure 1.3.

The annual percentage change in Figure 1.3 is easily calculated. For example, on June 6, 1998, the Dow was at 8,829 points. One year later on June 6, 1999, the Dow was at 10,841 points. Thus, the annual percentage change is $(10,841 - 8,829)/8,829 = 0.2279$ or 22.79%. This value is assigned to June 6, 1999.

Figure 1.3 shows that except for the early 1930s, when the Dow increased more than 150% and then decreased by more than 50%, the annual percentage change of the Dow has been between –50% and +60%. This percentage change method is a more realistic measure of the long-term development of the Dow, and it shows no sign of an unreasonable buying craze or irrational exuberance.

Comparing the Dow with the two other main indexes in the United States, the S&P 500 (Standard & Poor's 500) and the high-tech Nasdaq (National Association of Dealers Automated Quoting), we derive Figure 1.4. So why is the Dow the most widely followed index in the world? One reason is because it's the oldest index and

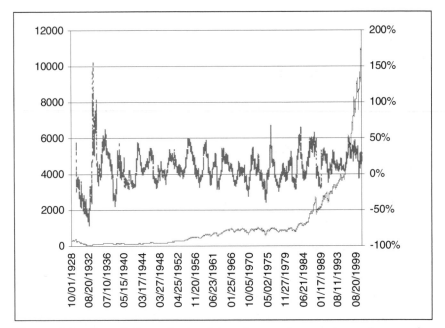

Figure 1.3   Dow (left vertical axis) and annual percentage change of the Dow (right vertical axis)

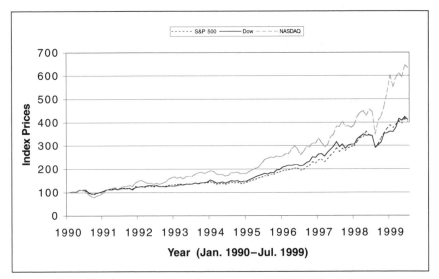

Figure 1.4   The Dow in comparison with the S&P 500 and the Nasdaq

it contains blue chip stocks, i.e., the most famous and historically successful companies in the U.S., such as Boeing, Coca-Cola, McDonalds, Walt Disney, General Motors, and IBM. (For a complete list of all current Dow stocks see Table 1.3.) Also, the Dow is handy, because it contains only 30 stocks, while the Nasdaq lists about 5000 stocks and the S&P covers 500 stocks. The Dow also has the lowest volatility of the three most quoted indixes, which means it carries the lowest risk. This is a crucial advantage. For a detailed discussion on volatility, see Chapter 6.

Mutual funds indexed to the Dow's rival, the S&P 500, may be one of the most popular investment vehicles, yet most investors who put their money into these funds probably cannot tell where the S&P index is within a thousand points. However, just about anybody who watches the news can probably tell how the Dow has been doing lately. As America's business barometer, the Dow provides a quick snapshot of the market's overall strength and represents about 20% of the U.S. stock market capitalization.

COMPOSITION OF THE DOW

As mentioned previously, in 1884 Charles H. Dow came up with the first list of eleven actively traded stocks, nine of which were railroads. In 1886 the first real version of twelve industrial stocks were quoted on a regular basis. The original Dow is listed in Table 1.1. The Dow was expanded to 30 stocks in October of 1928, just a year before the great crash.

The Dow's composition has been constantly changing over the years. Eastman Kodak Co. was added to the index in 1930, American Telephone & Telegraph Co. in 1939, International Paper Co. in 1956, Merck & Co. in 1979, Philip Morris Co. and McDonald's Corp. in 1985, and Boeing Co. joined in 1987.

Coca-Cola Co. made it into the Dow in 1932, only to get replaced three years later. It then spent half a century out of the Dow before rejoining the list in 1987. International Business Machines Corp. joined the list in 1932, was traded for American Telephone & Tele-

TABLE 1.1   Original Dow Dozen

Company	What Became of It
American Cotton Oil	Distant ancestor of CPC International
American Sugar	Evolved into Amstar Holdings
American Tobacco	Broken up in 1911 antitrust action
Chicago Gas	Absorbed by Peoples Gas, 1897
Distilling & Cattle Feeding	Evolved into Quantum Chemical
General Electric	Going strong and still listed in the Dow
Laclede Gas	Active, removed from Dow in 1899
National Lead	Today's NL Industries
Tennessee Coal & Iron	Absorbed by U.S. Steel in 1907
North American	Utility combine broken up in 1940s
U.S. Leather (preferred)	Dissolved in 1952
U.S. Rubber	Now part of Michelin

graph Co. seven years later, and then rejoined the Dow in 1979, when it became the market's bellwether stock. In 1991, Caterpillar Inc., Walt Disney Co., and J.P. Morgan & Co. entered the average while the struggling Navistar and the restructured USX Corp. were bumped and Primerica Corp. was given a respite.

The index has taken on more of a growth profile in recent years with the addition of Coca-Cola Co., Walt Disney Co., and other companies that don't fall prey to the traditional business cycle. The new additions continue to move the Dow away from historical industrial cyclical patterns and closer to world economic cycles.

On March 17, 1997, the editors at the *Wall Street Journal* changed the makeup of the Dow once again: Travelers Group Inc. replaced Westinghouse Electric Corp.; Hewlett-Packard Co. took the place of Texaco Inc.; Johnson & Johnson succeeded Bethlehem Steel Corp.; and Wal-Mart Stores Inc. moved into the spot vacated by F. W. Woolworth Co.

The changes were designed to lend greater weight to technology, health care, and finance, three increasingly important sectors of the U.S. economy. The catalyst for the update effort was Westinghouse's decision to spin off its industrial operations and become a pure play broadcaster. With the ABC and NBC networks already part of the Dow by way of Walt Disney Co. and General Electric Co., respectively, the new Westinghouse Electric Corp, which centers around the CBS network, became expendable.

Wal-Mart Stores Inc. has outperformed every other retailer, so they replaced F. W. Woolworth Co. Health Care accounts for about a seventh of the nation's economy, so the addition of the pharmaceutical giant Johnson & Johnson updates the average to include this major economic sector. Table 1.2 summarizes these recent changes.

On November 1, 1999, the Dow was again dramatically changed to prepare it for the twenty-first century. Companies included were the software giant Microsoft (even though it is being threatened by legal battles), Intel Corp., SBC Communications, and Home Depot. Chevron, Goodyear, Sears Roebuck and Union Carbide were forced out. The addition of Microsoft and Intel marked the first time that non-NYSE stocks were integrated into the Dow. (These two companies trade on the computerized high-tech Nasdaq.)

The latest alteration in the Dow was a clear recognition of the growing importance of technology in the U.S. economy. Before the change only IBM and Hewlett Packard were considered high-tech. With Microsoft, Intel, and SBC Communications, five out of the 30 companies that comprise the Dow are now high-tech.

The latest move also represents a shift from cheap value stocks toward expensive growth-oriented stocks. While the dropped Sears Corp. had a PE ratio of 8, its replacement, Home Depot, was fairly expensive with a PE of 55. This increased the average PE of the Dow from 21 to 25.

In November 1999, the capitalization of the Dow rose dramatically. The four new Dow companies had a capitalization of $977 billion. The departing members had an aggregate of a mere $82

TABLE 1.2   Recent changes in the Dow

Aug. 30, 1982	American Express Co. replaced Manville.
July 2, 1984	Standard Oil (Calif.) changed their name to Chevron.
Sept. 19, 1985	Allied Corp. changed their name to Allied-Signal Inc.
Oct. 30, 1985	Philip Morris Cos. and McDonald's Corp. were added. General Foods Corp. and American Brands Inc. were dropped.
Feb. 20, 1986	International Harvestor changed their name to Navistar International Corp.
July 8, 1986	U.S. Steel changed their name to USX Corp.
March 11, 1987	Inco and Owens-Illinois were dropped. Coca-Cola Co. and Boeing Co. were added.
April 29, 1987	American Can Co. changed their name to Primerica Corp.
Dec. 16, 1988	Primerica Corp. (old) merged into Commercial Credit Group Inc. which adopted Primerica Corp.'s name.
May 3, 1991	Caterpillar Inc., Walt Disney Co., and J.P. Morgan & Co. were added. Navistar International Corp., USX Corp., and Primerica Corp. were dropped.
March 14, 1997	Hewlett-Packard Co., Johnson & Johnson, Travelers Group Inc., and Wal-Mart Stores Inc. were added. Bethleham Steel Corp., Texaco Inc., Westinghouse Electric Corp., and F. W. Woolworth Corp. were dropped.
Oct. 8, 1998	Travelers Group Inc., changed its name to Citigroup Inc. (NYSE symbol C), following its merger with Citicorp.
Nov. 1, 1999	Microsoft, Intel Corp., SBC Communications, and Home Depot were added. Chevron, Goodyear, Sears Roebuck, and Union Carbide were dropped.

billion. This latest change is also likely to increase the volatility of the Dow, as growth stocks are usually more volatile than value stocks.

What becomes clear is that the Dow is a *performance-oriented* index. Only successful companies are included and retained. Therefore, the Dow is bound to outperform the market as a whole. It is only a matter of time until some of the high-flying Internet stocks will enter the Dow. AOL and Yahoo! are the most likely candidates to join the Dow during the next makeover.

Table 1.3 shows all companies of the Dow as of November 1, 1999, along with their current symbols.

Money is a terrible master, but a great servant.

—P. T. Barnum

CALCULATION OF THE DOW

Calculating the Dow is based on a relatively simple formula. The formula was adapted from Richard Stillman's Dow Jones Industrial Average (1986). As a price-weighted average, the index was originally calculated by adding up the total price of the Dow stocks and dividing by the number of stocks in the index.

For example, assume that the index consisted of only three stocks trading at $180, $120, and $60 per share, respectively. The numbers add up to $360, which divided by 3, returns a Dow value of 120. So the *divisor* is 3, meaning that a $1 increase in any stock increases the Dow by $1/3 = 0.33 points.

As stock prices increase, companies prefer to split the shares to keep the price within the market norms. This has two benefits: First, it ensures that investors can afford to buy the stocks, and second, it creates the illusion of a bargain. So, if the $180 stock splits two-for-one, the total would add up to just $90 + $120 + $60

TABLE 1.3   Stocks in the Dow as of November 1, 1999

Stocks in the Dow as of November 1, 1999	Current Symbol
Allied Signal Inc./Allied Corp.	ALD
Aluminum Co. of America	AA
American Express Co.	AXP
AT&T Corp.	T
Boeing Co.	BA
Caterpillar Inc.	CAT
Citigroup Inc./Travelers Group	C
Coca-Cola Co.	KO
DuPont Co.	DD
Eastman Kodak Co.	EK
Exxon Corp.	XON
General Electric Co.	GE
General Motors Corp.	GM
Hewlett-Packard Co.	HWP
Home Depot	HD
Intel Corp.	INTC
International Business Machines Corp.	IBM
International Paper Co.	IP
J.P. Morgan & Co.	JPM
Johnson & Johnson	JNJ
McDonald's Corp.	MCD
Merck & Co.	MRK
Microsoft	MSFT
Minnesota Mining & Manufacturing Co.	MMM
Philip Morris Cos./General Foods Corp.	MO
Procter & Gamble Co.	PG
SBC Communications	SBC
United Technologies Corp.	UTX
Wal-Mart Stores Inc.	WMT
Walt Disney Co.	DIS

= \$270, even though the real value of the stocks remained exactly the same.

To solve the split dilemma, we have to change the divisor. The new divisor is the total after-stock-split Dow value divided by the before-stock-split average, thus \$270/\$120 = 2.25. Now every \$1 increase in any stock increases the Dow by \$1/2.25 = 0.44 points. Over the years, more and more stocks have split and the divisor has decreased steadily and turned into a multiplier. This means that every \$1 increase in any stock increases the Dow by more than 1 point. As of July 10, 1998, the divisor for the Dow was 0.24275214, which means that every one dollar change in any Dow stock is worth a 4.11942815-point change in the Dow (\$1/0.24275214 = 4.11942815). In other words, a \$5 per share increase in Merck & Co., Inc. will boost the Dow more than 20 points.

Because the Dow is a *price-weighted* average, there are some important aspects that must be noted. First, a 10% increase in a higher-priced stock will actually raise the index more than a similar increase in a lower-priced stock. For example, a 10% increase in Walt Disney Co., currently trading at about \$30 dollars a share, would boost the average by 12.36 points (3/0.24275214). However, a 10% jump in Merck & Co., Inc.'s stock, currently trading at about \$130 a share, would add 53.55 points to the index (13/0.24275214). It is also important to note that if Merck & Co., Inc. were to split two-for-one so that it traded for around \$75 a share, the identical 10% price appreciation would now be worth only about 31 points (7.5/0.24275214). Of course, the divisor would be changed by the Merck & Co., Inc. stock split, but that change would not be enough to compensate for the specific alteration in the pricing of Merck & Co., Inc. stock.

Dividends and the Dow

Dividends are distributions by companies to shareholders, usually paid in the form of cash. In rare cases, the dividend payment is made in the form of stocks, scrip, or company product. In the U.S. dividends are paid quarterly; in Europe and in Asia they are usually paid annually.

Any calculation of the appreciation of a portfolio made up of Dow stocks must take into account the impact of dividends. During the bull market of recent years, many investors have almost forgotten about any return on their stock holdings from dividend payments; stock price gains have been the name of the game. Several high tech stocks, for example, Microsoft, Cisco, and AOL, don't even pay a dividend. However, historically, dividends have provided more than 40% of the stock market's total return. The figure has been about half that over the last 20 years and is currently down to about 10%.

Dividend payments are usually measured as a percentage of the stock price. So if Boeing trades at $100 and pays a $1 dividend, the dividend yield is $1/$100 = 0.01, or 1%. Table 1.4 shows the dividend yields of the Dow since 1905.

Through the payment of dividends, mature companies share the wealth with the investors who hold their stock. Companies often pursue a dividend policy of steadily increasing the dividend to ensure confidence in the company. Some companies strive mightily to increase their dividends on a regular basis, even when their earnings may actually decrease. Of course, this can't go on for long, because companies need to return some of their profits to the business in order to modernize their production operations and fund research and development efforts that will guarantee a steady line of improved products.

Companies do not reduce their dividends unless they really must. A reduction of dividends is considered an extremely bad sign of the company's overall performance and is usually followed by a sharp decline in the stock price. Dow companies that totally fail to pay dividends are usually removed from the Dow at the next available opportunity, as was the case with Bethlehem Steel Corp. and F. W. Woolworth Co.

TABLE 1.4   Dividend Yield Range for the Dow Since 1905

Record high (1932)	16.6%
Average yield of ten highest yielding stocks in the Dow	6.5%
Average yield of the Dow	4.3%
Average yield of ten lowest yielding stocks in the Dow	3.0%
Record Low (1998)	2.2%

Just as the Dow is adjusted for stock splits, the Dow is also adjusted for dividend payments. The mechanics are as follows:

> *A stock decreases in price on the ex-dividend date by the amount of the dividend. For example, if IBM announces a $2 dividend and the ex-dividend date is June 24, then the stock will drop by $2 on June 24 (on top of the price movement due to supply and demand on June 24). The payment of the $2 dividend to the shareholder is usually three weeks after the ex-dividend date.*
>
> *On June 24, the Dow is adjusted for the $2 fall in IBM. Let's assume the divisor is 0.5. Therefore, the $2 drop in the IBM means a $2/0.5 = $4 drop in the Dow. Let's say before the split the Dow was at 10,000. Thus, after the split the Dow is at 9,996. To raise the Dow back to 10,000 we have to multiply by 10,000/9,996 = 1.0004. This will bring the Dow back to its pre-split level (9,996 × 1,0004 = 10,000). In this example, the divisor has changed from 0.5 to 1.0004 × 0.5 = 0.5002.*

SUMMARY

In 1884, Charles H. Dow came up with the first list of eleven actively traded stocks, and published them in the "Customer's Afternoon Letter", a forerunner to the *The Wall Street Journal*. Since then the Dow has become a remarkable success story. From a low of 28.48 in 1886, the Dow has risen to break 10,000 in March 1999. Historically, the Dow has suffered two big crashes. After excessive exuberance in the late 1920s, in October 1929 panic selling set in, which led to the Great Depression of the early 1930s. On October 24, 1987, the Dow suffered its biggest percentage loss of 22.6%. However, unlike 1929, the market soon stabilized and regained all its losses by 1989. In the 1990s steady economic growth and increased stock market awareness fueled a steady Dow increase. In percentage terms, the Dow has shown a powerful, but not excessive rise.

The Dow is a performance-oriented index: Unsuccessful companies are removed from the Dow, profitable companies are added in
their place. This assures a successful future for the Dow. IBM and
Coca-Cola are the two stocks that were removed from the Dow due
to poor performance and later reinstated when profitability
increased.

The most recent changes to the Dow were made in November
1999: Chevron, Goodyear, Sears Roebuck, and Union Carbide were
eliminated from the Dow. Newcomers to the Dow were Microsoft,
Intel Corp., SBC Communications, and Home Depot. These
changes increased the high-technology component of the Dow and
also represented a shift from cheap value stocks to fairly expensive
growth-oriented stocks. Due to the changes, the market capitalization of the Dow rose by $895 billion.

The Dow is a price-weighted average. Thus, a 10% increase in
an expensive stock has a higher impact on the Dow than a 10%
increase in a cheaper stock. A divisor, which is actually a multiplier,
adjusts the Dow for stock splits and dividends. The dividend yield
(dividend divided by stock price) of the stocks in the Dow has been
steadily decreasing. Profit derived from stock price increases are
now the major reward that Dow stockholders receive.

SUGGESTED READING

Birinyi, L., "Okay I'm boring," *Forbes,* 162(3), 1998, p. 125.

Gardner, D., Tom Gardner, (1996). *The Motley Fool Investment Guide: How
the fool beats Wall Street's wise men and how you can too,* (New York:
Simon and Schuster).

"The History of the Dow Jones Industrial Average (log-log)," Dow Jones &
Company. In honor of the 100th anniversary of the Dow Jones Industrial Average. http://home.san.rr.com/ecandmg/djia.html

Kadlec, D. (1997). "The Dogs of the Dow Won't Hunt," *Time,* 150(24), p. 76.

Lynch, P., John Rothchild, (1989). *One Up on Wall Street: How to Use What
You Know to Make Money in the Market,* (New York: Simon and
Schuster).

Mader, C., R. Hagin, (1996). "The Dow Jones-Irwin Guide to Common
Stocks," (Homewood, IL: Dow Jones-Irwin).

Malkin B., (1996). *A Random Walk Down Walk Street,* (New York: W. W. Norton & Company).

Morton, J., (1995). "Global Guide to Investing," *Financial Times* (London).

Norton, R., (1999). *Investing for Income,* (New York: McGraw-Hill).

O'Higgens, M., John Downes, (1991). *Beating the Dow: A High-Return, Low-Risk Method for Investing in the Dow Jones Industrial Stocks with as Little as $5,000,* (New York: HarperCollins Publishers).

Sheimo, M., (1993). *Stock Market Rules,* (New York: Probus Publishing Co.)

Stillman R., (1986). "Dow Jones Industrial Average: History and Role in the Investment Strategy," (Homewood, IL: Dow Jones-Irwin).

2

METHODS TO PREDICT STOCK PRICES: AN OVERVIEW

The predictions of experts are usually not much worse than those of laymen.

FUNDAMENTAL ANALYSIS

A leading method for predicting stock prices is *fundamental analysis*. Fundamental analysis involves trying to forecast the movement of a stock price based on political, economic, sector-specific, and company-specific data.

Political Stability

The political stability of a country influences investor behavior and stock prices. Only invest in countries with a stable democracy! Furthermore, a strong government based on a healthy majority in the Upper and Lower House usually has a positive influence on stock prices. In addition, conservative parties in power are usually more welcomed by stock markets than left wing parties.

Macro-economic Data

Macro-economic data also have an important influence on stock prices. For example, the inflation numbers consumer price index (CPI) and producer price index (PPI) should be closely observed. A high CPI and PPI lead to higher bond yields, and therefore favor bonds relative to stocks. High interest rates as a result of high inflation also lead to higher discount factors. These discount factors are used to discount the future earnings of a company and thus decrease the fair present value of a stock with negative effects on stock prices.

The *gross domestic product (GDP)* growth rate is an indicator for potential earnings of a company. A stable, moderate GDP growth rate of 2% to 4% is considered healthy for a stock market. A low growth rate lowers earnings expectations; a high growth rate spurs inflation fears. Both have negative effects on the stock market.

The *unemployment rate* is an important economic indicator. Due to migration of workers, an unemployment rate of 4% to 5% is considered full employment. A high unemployment rate, as seen currently in Europe, indicates structural problems in the economy. The unemployment rate is, however, a lagging indicator. It decreases after the economic expansion is well on its way and increases after a recession has already occurred. The unemployment rate is therefore not a good predictor for future stock movements.

The *employment cost index* (ECI) is an indicator that Federal Reserve Board chairman Alan Greenspan carefully observes. The employment cost index measures the change in wages, salaries, and benefits and is not influenced by employment shifts among occupations and industries. It is therefore considered a good measurement for accelerating or decelerating wage pressures and consequently, an important indicator for future inflation.

In the recent past, *mutual fund capital inflow* has become an extremely important indicator for the stock market. The astonishing rally of the Dow in the 1990s is, to a high degree, due to more capital being invested in stocks, especially for retirement purposes. For example, in 1990 the percentage of households investing in stocks in the United States was 20%. In 1996 this percentage was 43%. The future development of the stock market therefore depends highly on the degree of future capital inflow.

Other important macro-economic indicators are durable goods orders, industrial production, construction spending, housing starts, home sales, retail sales, consumer confidence, the beige book, leading indicators, national association of purchasing managers index (NAPM), trade balance, and budget deficit.

Sector

The sector you invest in is also of great importance. If you invest in a mature economy like that of the United States, don't invest heavily in declining sectors such as agriculture and industrial production. The sectors that promise higher returns are the expanding sectors such as the service industry or the high-tech industry. The Nasdaq (an index of about 5,000 high-tech stocks) has outperformed both the Dow and S&P 500 in recent years.

Company-specific Data

Before buying the stock of a company, company-specific data should be analyzed. One of the most important ratios is the *price-earnings ratio (PE)*. The PE is the price of the stock divided by the earnings per share of the company. The earnings in the PE ratio can be trailing, current, or expected. If the company is healthy and earnings are growing, the trailing PE ratio is higher than the current PE ratio, which is again higher than the expected (also called forward) PE ratio. The PE, which is published in newspapers and online, is usually the expected PE. As an example, if the stock of a company trades at $100 and next year's expected earnings per share is $5, then the expected PE ratio is 20. Naturally, the lower the PE ratio, the cheaper the stock, and vice versa. As of June 1999, a PE ratio of 22 can be considered average in the U.S. High-tech stocks as Microsoft (PE 73) or Dell (PE 64) can have much higher PE ratios than the index. This shows the high earnings expectations of these fast growing companies.

Also of importance is the *earnings per share* ratio. It shows the allocation of the earnings to each share. For example, if the earnings last year were $10 million and the number of outstanding stock is 10 million shares, the earnings per share is $1. This number is calculated after deducting taxes and dividends from the earnings.

Closely related to the earnings per share ratio is the *return on equity* ratio. It shows how profitable each share is. Return on equity is calculated as the return (= earnings) divided by the common stock at par + capital surplus + retained earnings. (The par price of a stock is the original issue price of the stock.) Capital surplus is the difference between the current stock price and the par stock price that the company achieves for sold stocks. Unlike the earnings per share, which is expressed in dollars, the return on equity is expressed as a percentage. For example, if the yearly return of a company is $1,000,000, and the sum of common stock at par + capital surplus + retained earnings is $10,000,000, the return on equity is 10%.

Another important ratio is the *dividend yield*. It is the yearly dividend divided by the current price of the stock. For example, if the dividend per year is $2 and the price of the stock is $100, then the dividend yield is 2%. High tech stocks like Microsoft and Dell often do not pay a dividend. Investors buy these stocks because of the expected price appreciation.

Other important ratios are:

- debt-equity ratio = (bonds + preferred stock) divided by (common stock at par + capital surplus + retained earnings)
- net working capital ratio = total current assets divided by total current liabilities
- cash flow ratio = net income (or loss) + annual depreciation
- operating profit margin = operating income divided by net sales

TECHNICAL ANALYSIS

Technical analysis is not voodoo, or is it?

An increasingly popular way to predict stock prices is *technical analysis*. Technical analysis is trying to forecast the movement of a stock price by observing the pattern it has followed in the past.

Technical analysis belongs to the field of heuristics, the non-mathematical way of finding a solution. Due to its heuristic nature, technical analysis can hardly be proven theoretically. In addition, technical analysis is difficult to prove empirically, due to its highly subjective nature.

Despite these drawbacks, technical analysis has become extremely popular in the 1990s. Even critics cannot ignore the relevance of technical analysis due to "self fulfilling prophecy"—the fact that many traders act according to technical analysis is exactly why the theory is becoming more and more accurate in forecasting market movements.

The Philosophy of Technical Analysis

Technical analysis is based on three crucial assumptions:

1. Chart patterns reflect the fundamental data in an economy or a company.
2. The markets move in trends.
3. History repeats itself.

Chart Patterns Reflect the Fundamental Data   This first assumption that chart patterns reflect the fundamental data is necessary in order to include fundamental data in the theory of technical analysis. It is obviously quite a presumptuous assumption and it is not surprising that it has become the main area of criticism. Nevertheless, technical analysts (or also called chartists) do assume that fundamental data such as GDP growth, inflation, unemployment, and company-specific data such as earnings expectations or price earnings ratios are reflected in the supply and demand for a security, which determines the price movement of that security. Because technical analysts believe that fundamental data is inherent in chart formations, technical analysts are principally not interested in the fundamental data itself.

It is obvious that exogenous shocks, such as unforeseeable political events or natural disasters, are not included in chart patterns and can lead to an unexpected reversal of an established pattern. However, the fact that exogenous shocks are unforseeable is also a problem when trading according to the theory of fundamental analysis.

The trend is your friend.

The Market Moves in Trends   The second assumption of technical analysis is that markets move in trends. A *trend* is the direction in which a market moves. An *upward trend* (see Figure 2.1) is a movement with consecutively higher lows and consecutively higher highs. A *downward trend* is a movement with consecutively lower lows and consecutively lower highs. A *sideward trend* is a movement that does not exceed a certain high and does not fall below a certain low.

The existence of trends is absolutely crucial for technical analysts, because most theories of technical analysis try to identify a trend and the trend-reversal and then recommend exploiting it (buy in an upward trend and sell in an downward trend).

In order to create a trend pattern, the time horizon and the frequency of price selection is important. Short-term trends can be as short as minutes, super-long trends can be as long as 50 or 100 years. Price selection can be based on every executed trade price or daily closing prices.

Due to differences in time horizon and frequency of price selection, the movement of the same variable can result in very differ-

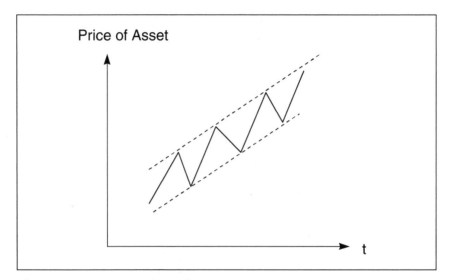

Figure 2.1 An upward trend

ent looking patterns. A longer time horizon and a more frequent price selection might establish an upward trend, whereas a shorter time horizon and a price selection based on daily closing prices might not show an upward trend. This reflects the highly subjective nature of technical analysis.

Nevertheless, basically all traders will agree that markets often move in some form of trend. Therefore, this assumption is not a major criticism of technical analysis.

History Repeats Itself Technical analysis assumes that human behavior is repetitive. Indeed, studies in psychology suggest that it is human nature to repeat a strategy that has worked in the past.

Furthermore, the study of market patterns in the last 100 years shows that certain market movements have occurred on a regular basis. Therefore the assumption that patterns are repetitive has not been a major criticism of the technical analysis approach.

There are numerous theories of technical analysis that are applied in trading. The main theories will be discussed in the following section.

Theories of Technical Analysis

Don't fight the market forces, use them.

Point and Figure Chart   There are three main ways of plotting a price movement: A line chart, a bar chart, and a point and figure chart.

The line chart simply combines the quoted prices in a graph. These prices can consist of every traded price, traded prices on a half-hourly or hourly basis, daily, weekly, or monthly closing prices. The bar chart plots the highest and lowest trading price of the relevant time period (usually a day) and sometimes the opening price or closing price. Figure 2.2 shows a sample bar chart.

The main difference between line and bar charts and a point and figure chart is that the point and figure chart considers time irrelevant. The only determinant for building the chart is the price action.

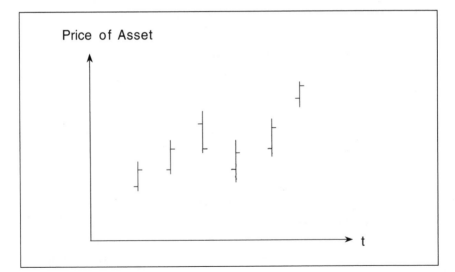

Figure 2.2   In this bar chart, the horizontal lines to the left represent the opening price and the ones to the right represent the closing price

The purpose of the point and figure chart is (as with most theories of technical analysis), to identify a trend and the trend reversal.

Construction of a Point and Figure Chart: The point and figure chart does not use lines or bars to represent a price movement, but uses an "x" for an upward movement and an "o" for a downward movement. Furthermore, two elements are important for the construction of the chart, the box size and the reversal. The *box size* represents the necessary change of the price in order to draw a new "x" or "o." The bigger the box size, the more insensitive the graph is to price movements, and vice versa. The *reversal* represents the necessary change of the price in order to begin a new column. The bigger the reversal, the less frequently a new column will be created and therefore, trend reversals will occur less often and vice versa.

EXAMPLE 2.1 *Let's assume the following price action:*

Day:	1	2	3	4	5	6	7	8	9	10
Price:	50	55	65	67	68	55	50	60	65	70

Let's choose 5 as the box size and 10 as the reversal. The point and figure graph shown in Figure 2.3 is then generated:

For day 2 one "x" is drawn at 55, because the market has risen by the amount of one box size. For day 3 two "x's" are drawn in the same column at 60 and 65, because the market has moved up by twice the box size. For day 4 and day 5, the point and figure chart is not altered, because the market has changed by less than the box size. On day 6 the market drops by more than the reversal. Therefore two "o's" are drawn in a new column. On day 7 the market drops by the box size, so another "o" is drawn in the same column. On day 8 the market changes by the reversal, so two "x's" are drawn in a new column. On days 9 and 10 the market rises by the box size, so for each day an "x" is drawn in the same column.

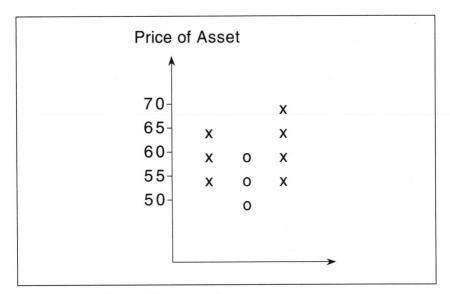

Figure 2.3   Point and figure graph

Note that in Figure 2.3 that the x-axis is dimensionless.

Due to its simplicity, the point and figure chart is widely used in order to identify a trend and the trend reversal. An upward trend is intact as long as x's are drawn. A downward trend is intact as long as o's are drawn. A new upward trend starts when a new column of x's is drawn. A new downward trend starts when a new column of o's is drawn. One drawback of the point and figure chart is that different box sizes and reversals lead to different trend identifications for the same price movement.

Simple Chart Patterns   We will now explain the most widely used reversal and continuation patterns.

■ Definition

Support and Resistance: A *support level* is a level where the market is expected to stop dropping, and possibly reverse upwards. However, if the support level is broken to the downside, a further significant drop can be expected. A *resistance level* is a level where the market is expected to stop rising, and possibly reverse downwards. However, if the resistance is broken to the upside, a further significant rise can be expected.

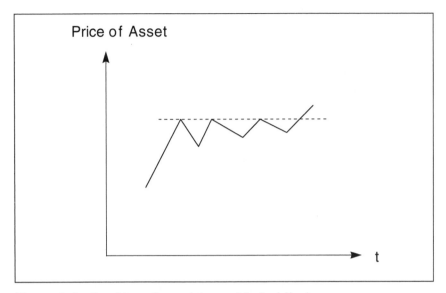

Figure 2.4 Breaking of a resistance (dashed line)

It should be noted that a *significant* breaking of a support or resistance is considered necessary in order to call the levels broken. This is because stop losses (a level where a buyer cuts his or her losses and sells, or a seller cuts his or her losses and buys) are usually placed somewhat beneath a support or somewhat above a resistance. Therefore, significant breaking means a move of one to five ticks, or bips (the smallest trading unit) above the resistance or below the support.

One simple way to identify support and resistance levels is to look at previous highs and lows, which are considered indicative of support and resistance levels for the future (see Figure 2.5).

Figure 2.6 shows another simple way to identify support and resistance levels. The previous lows are connected. The resultant line is considered a support line.

Support and resistance levels develop opposite roles after they have been violated. This means that, once they have been broken, a support turns into a resistance and a resistance into a support (see Figure 2.7).

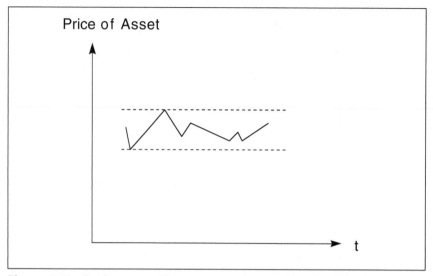

Figure 2.5   Resistance and support as the previous low and high

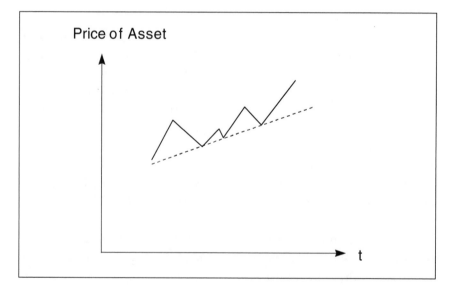

Figure 2.6   A support line, created by connecting previous lows

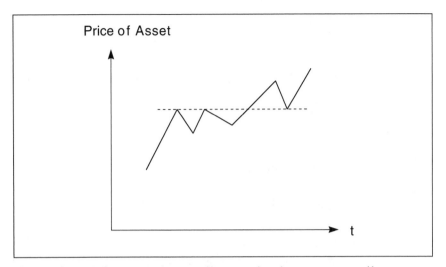

Figure 2.7 A former resistance line turning into a support line

Because technical analysis is not based on mathematical equations but on rules mainly derived by psychology, it is obvious that these rules may fail. Figure 2.8 shows a false breakout. The resistance is broken significantly, but the market does not continue to

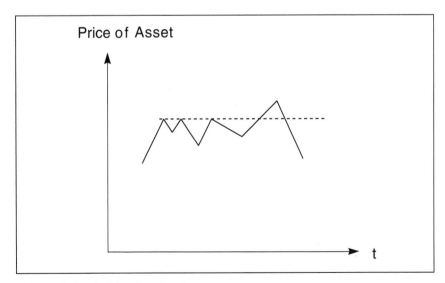

Figure 2.8 A false breakout

rise. Naturally, a false breakout to the downside is possible. In that case, a support line is broken, but the market does not continue to fall.

Altogether, due to their simplicity, support and resistance lines are among the most popular technical instruments. They serve as a basis for most theories in technical analysis. They tend to work well in basically all liquid markets.

Double Tops, Double Bottoms, Triple Tops, Triple Bottoms, and Flags   Easy to recognize formations are double tops, also called M-formations and double bottoms, also called W-formations. They are reversal patterns, inclined to show the end of an old and the beginning of a new trend.

In an ideal double top formation, as shown in Figure 2.9, the market increases to point "a," usually on high volume, and retreats to "b." Then the market moves back up to "c." So far, the formation is still in line with an upward trend. Now however, the market fails to break the resistance "B," drops, and breaks the support line "A"

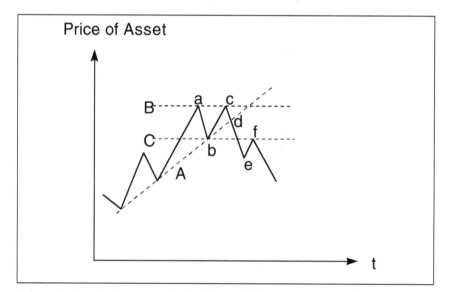

Figure 2.9   An ideal double top formation

at point "d." It also breaks a potential support line "C," so the market does not establish a sideward trend. After reaching point "e," the market might retreat to "f." Not breaking the resistance line "C" (which was formerly a support line), the market retreats further and establishes a downward trend.

Double bottoms work exactly the opposite, with volume usually increasing when the market reverts to the upside.

Triple tops and triple bottoms show an even stronger reversal of a trend. Triple tops can occur with three highs at similar levels (see Figure 2.10).

If the second high is the highest, it is called a Head and Shoulders formation. Figure 2.11 shows an ideal Head and Shoulders formation. This formation might occur when a market has been in an upward trend for a while. However it begins losing momentum and a downward trend is then established.

Until point "c" the upward trend is still intact, because "b" is higher than the previous low and "c" is higher than "a." Now, however, the market breaks the support line "A" and falls to "d." The

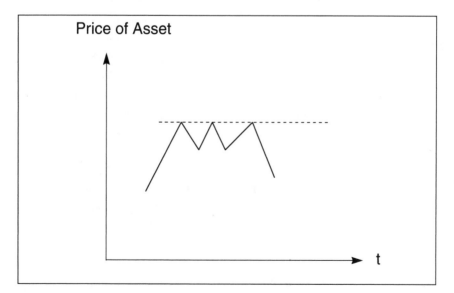

Figure 2.10 Triple top formation

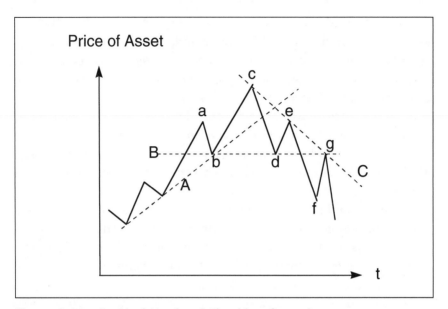

Figure 2.11 An ideal Head and Shoulders formation

market reverts to "e" but then falls to "f," breaking the "neckline B." This breaking of the neckline is considered crucial in a Head and Shoulders formation (which is also true from a biological point of view). The market might now test the former support neckline "B," which has turned into a resistance at point "g," but fails to break it, and a downward trend is established. A new resistance line "C" is established by connecting the previous highs "c," "e," and "g." A trend reversal via a Head and Shoulders usually occurs on increasing volume.

It is obvious that an ideal Head and Shoulders formation such as Figure 2.11 is seldom found in reality. It is up to the chartist to judge whether a pattern that violates some features of a Head and Shoulders formation still qualifies as such a formation. Here again the subjective nature of chart analysis comes into play.

As to be expected, a reverse Head and Shoulders formation exists in technical analysis, which would indicate a reversal of a downward trend, and therefore a good buying opportunity.

Another interesting chart formation is the flag, which illustrates a consolidation (sideward movement) in an upward or a downward trend. Figure 2.12 shows an ideal flag formation. The upward breakout indicates the start of an upward trend. The flag is usually short dated (up to three weeks) and occurs on low volume. For the breakout to be crucial, it should occur on high volume and the magnitude of the breakout should be significant in relation to the size of the flag.

Naturally, flag formations with a downward breakout indicate the start of a downward trend.

Moving Average Convergence/Divergence (MACD)   The Moving Average Convergence/Divergence (MACD) uses three exponentially smoothed averages to identify a trend reversal or the continuation of a trend.

The indicator, which was developed by Gerald Appel, reduces to two averages. The first, called the MACD1 indicator, is the difference between two exponential averages, usually a 26-day and a 12-

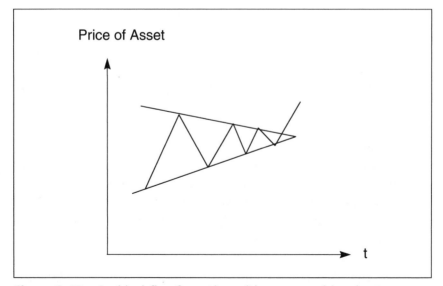

Figure 2.12   An ideal flag formation with an upward breakout

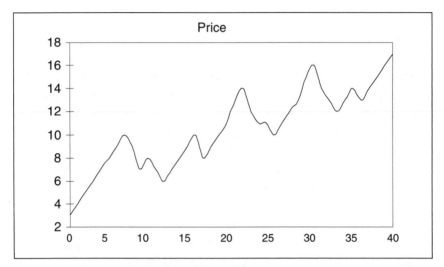

Figure 2.13   Price movement of a stock

day average. The second, called the Signal indicator, is the 9-day moving average of the MACD1 indicator.

The terms convergence and divergence refer to a narrowing and widening of the MACD1 and the Signal indicator: A buy signal is given when the more volatile average, the MACD1 indicator, crosses the less volatile average, the Signal indicator, from beneath. If the MACD1 line crosses the Signal line from above, a sell signal is given.

Let's look at an example. The 40-day price movement is shown in Figure 2.13.

From the stock price movement in Figure 2.13 we get the moving averages shown in Figure 2.14.

From Figure 2.14 we see that the three buy signals B_1, B_2, and B_3, worked well. The stock price in Figure 2.13 increases after each buy signal, especially after buy signal B_1.

The sell signals S_1, S_2, and S_3, also give the correct sell recommendations. The stock prices in Figure 2.13 decline after each sell signal; however, only briefly after sell signal S_3.

It is important to point out that a *significant* crossing of the two lines is necessary in order to indicate the beginning of a new trend.

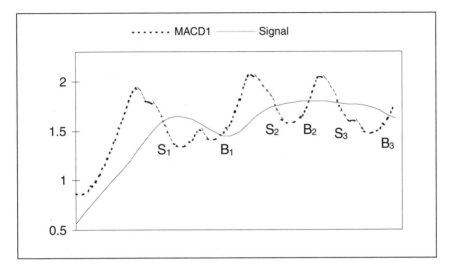

Figure 2.14 MACD 1 and Signal indicators resulting from Figure 2.13

Also, the closer the angle of crossing is to 90 degrees, the more crucial the crossing. A long parallel movement of the MACD1 and the Signal line with an occasional crossing is not considered an indication of a new trend.

A minor drawback of moving averages is that they are lagging indicators. They indicate a new trend after it has begun. This can be observed in Figures 2.13 and 2.14. The buy and sell signals are given some time *after* a new trend has already started.

The exponential moving average (EMA) is calculated as:

$$EMA_t = (P_t\,K - EMA_{t-1}\,K) + EMA_{t-1}$$

where

EMA_t = current value of exponential moving average

P_t = current price of underlying asset

K = 2/(number of periods + 1)

The previous equation implicitly includes the exponential smoothing: An $EMA_{t-1} = 10$, $K = 0.2$, (number of periods is 9), and a current price $P_t = 12$ leads to an EMA_t of 10.4. A price $P_t = 8$ leads to $EMA_t = 9.6$; a price $P_t = 4$ leads to an $EMA_t = 8.8$.

It should be mentioned that different time horizons, hourly versus 200-day moving averages, lead to different trend indications. It is up to the trader to decide which time horizon is best suited for the market he trades in, and for his performance time frame.

Altogether, moving averages work well in trending markets and are therefore a popular technical analysis tool.

Fibonacci Ratios and Elliot Wave Principle   In the thirteenth century the mathematician Fibonacci discovered a number series with some quite astonishing results.

Adding two numbers to derive a result, then taking the last added number and adding it to the result, gives:

> 1+1=2; 1+2=3; 2+3=5; 3+5=8 and so on,
> which gives the number series
> 2,3,5,8,13,21,34,55,89,144,....

Dividing consecutive numbers in this series by one another: 13/21, 21/34, 34/55, 55/89, 89/144 and so on, all yields the same result of 0.618 or 61.8%. Dividing a number by the one following two places behind, 13/34; 21/55; 34/89; 55/144, also yields a constant result of 0.382 or 38.2%. Some scientists believe that 61.8% and 38.2% are crucial numbers, which are supposed to occur in other sciences, natural phenomena, and human behavior. Technical analysts also consider these numbers crucial.

The Fibonacci numbers are integrated in certain theories of technical analysis. For instance, they are the mathematical basis for the *Elliot Wave Principle.* In 1946 the retired accountant Ralph Elliot wrote his book *Nature's Law—The Secret of the Universe.* The secret he gave to his descendants is the Elliot Wave Principle. In its most basic form, the principle says that markets move in a repetitive cycle of five waves to the upside (wave 1 through 5) followed by three waves to the downside (waves a to c). Waves 1, 3, 5 are called impulse waves, and waves 2 and 4 are called corrective waves (see Figure 2.15).

Elliot set three rules for his principle, which are necessary for a given pattern to qualify as an Elliot wave:

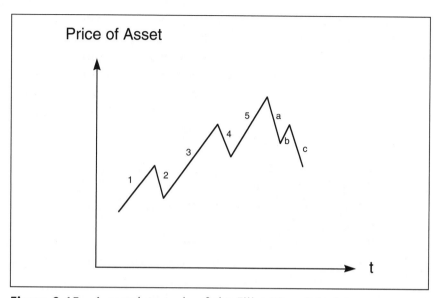

Figure 2.15 A complete cycle of the Elliot Wave Principle

1. Correction wave 2 can never retrace more than 100% of wave 1.
2. Wave 3 can never be the shortest wave of waves 1, 3, or 5.
3. The bottom of wave 4 is higher than the peak of wave 1.

Elliot also set less strict rules, which are not absolutely necessary for a wave to qualify as an Elliot wave. Here, the Fibonacci ratios come into play.

- The minimum length of wave 3 is the length of wave 1 plus 61.8% of wave 1.
- Wave 4 should reverse to the upside, after having retraced 38.2% of wave 3.
- The maximum length of wave 5 is multiplying the distance from the low of wave 1 and the high of wave 3 by 1.618.
- Highs and lows of the Elliot wave can be expected on days 13, 21, 34, 55, and 89.

The waves "a," "b," and "c" reflect the end of the five-wave upward trend. Crucial for the establishment of a new downward trend is that the low of wave "a" is lower than the high of wave 3. Wave "b" is a correction within the downward trend but fails to break the high of wave 3. Wave "c" underlines the new downward trend, breaking the low of wave 4. Waves 4, 5, a, b, and c strongly resemble a Head and Shoulders formation (see Figure 2.11).

The advantage the Elliot wave principle has over the MACD1 indicator is that it is not a lagging indicator. It is a leading indicator that attempts to pinpoint a market reversal before it has actually happened.

The disadvantage of the Elliot wave principle is its somewhat cumbersome nature. Due to the rules, recommendations, and possible variations, the degree of variability in identifying a pattern as an Elliot wave is quite large. Nevertheless, the Elliot wave principle is popular in the market and it has empirical evidence.

The Relative Strength Index (RSI)   The Relative Strength Index (RSI) was developed by Welles Wilder in 1978. It is based on the assumption that after a strong rally, the market is overbought and will enter into a downward correction phase. Similarly, after a strong fall, the market is assumed to be oversold and it will enter into an upward correction phase. The RSI tries to measure the degree of "overboughtness" and "oversoldness" and tries to identify when the correction phase is likely to begin.

Similarly to the theories previously discussed, the RSI works best in markets that have consecutive upward and downward trends. The use of the RSI in markets that keep rising long-term or falling long-term is not recommended.

The RSI is calculated as:

$$RSI = 100 - \{100/[1 + (Avg\ Up/Avg\ Dn)]\}$$

where

Avg Up = Sum of all changes for advancing periods divided by total of periods.

Avg Dn = Sum of all changes for declining periods divided by total of periods.

EXAMPLE 2.2

Day	1	2	3	4	5	6
Market close	100	103	106	101	99	103

Given these data, Avg Up = (3 + 3 + 4)/5 = 2
Avg Dn = (5 + 2)/5 = 1.4
According to the RSI equation,
$$RSI = 100 - (100/(1 + 1.43) = 58.85$$

According to the RSI equation, the RSI can take values between 0 and 100. The higher the RSI, the more the market is overbought, and vice versa. Therefore, in the above example, 58.85 means that the market is slightly overbought.

Figure 2.16 shows a 40-day price movement of a stock, and Figure 2.17 shows the resulting 10-day RSI. Generally, an RSI above 70 indicates an overbought market, which is likely to correct to the downside. An RSI of lower than 30 reflects an oversold market, which is likely to revert to the upside.

Figure 2.17 shows that the sell signal, S_1, works fine, as the stock price in Figure 2.16 decreases after the signal. The buy signal, B, also works well, as the price in Figure 2.16 increases after the signal. The sell signal, S_2, does not work too well because the stock price moves up to 16 before falling to 12, as seen in Figure 2.16.

Like other theories of technical analysis, the frequency of price selection and the time horizon is crucial. The RSI usually uses closing prices. Depending on the time horizon though, different lengths of the observed period obviously can lead to different RSIs. Here again, the subjective nature of technical analysis can be seen.

Altogether, the RSI is a popular tool which makes sense from an intuitive point of view: Traders that have gone long (bought the

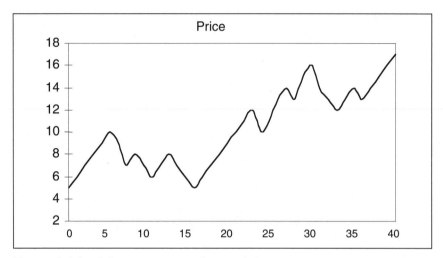

Figure 2.16   Price movement of a stock

security), tend to realize the profits and sell after a rally so that the market will correct, and vice versa.

As mentioned earlier, the reader should be aware that RSIs don't work in non-trending markets. In a strong bull market, an

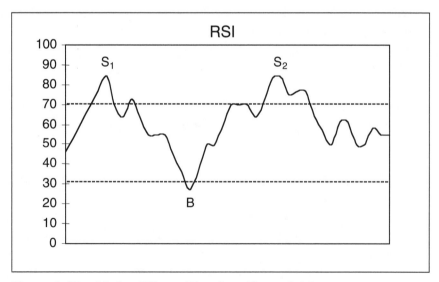

Figure 2.17   10-day RSI resulting from Figure 2.16

overbought situation with an RSI over 70 might occur for as long as the upward trend exists.

Momentum   One of the most simple theories of technical analysis is the *momentum analysis*. This theory tries to capture the strength of the price movement. The higher the momentum, the stronger the upward trend; the lower the momentum, the stronger the downward trend.

The momentum is simply calculated as the difference between the latest closing price, P_t, and the closing price x periods ago, P_x.

$$Momentum = P_t - P_x$$

x is often chosen to be 10 periods (usually 10 days), but 9 periods are also common. Critical for the momentum analysis is the crossing of the zero line. If the zero line is broken from above, a downward trend has started, if the zero line is broken from beneath, an upward trend has started.

Figure 2.18 shows a 40-day stock price movement and Figure 2.19 shows the resulting 10-day momentum. In Figure 2.19 we get a sell signal S when the zero line is crossed from the top. This signal does not work too well because the price in Figure 2.18 goes back up soon after signal S. Buy signal B in Figure 2.19 works well, as prices in Figure 2.18 move up strongly after the signal.

Stochastics   The stochastics indicator shows the position of the current stock price relative to past price range. If the stock is caught in a sideways trend, a high stochastic number represents a sell signal. Conversely, a low stochastic number indicates a buy signal.

Stochastics uses two indicators, K and D. K is calculated as:

$$K = 100 \times (P_t - L_5)/(H_5 - L_5)$$

where
P_t = latest (often closing) price
L_5 = lowest price of past five days
H_5 = highest price of the last five days

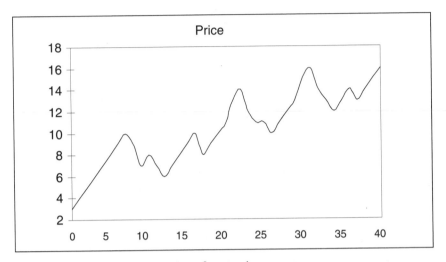

Figure 2.18 Price movement of a stock

D is the 3-day moving average of K. This reminds us of the MACD indicator, where the signal indicator is the 9-day moving average of the MACD1 indicator.

Figures 2.20 and 2.21 show a 40-day stock price movement and the resulting 10-day stochastics. If the indicator D is above 80, this

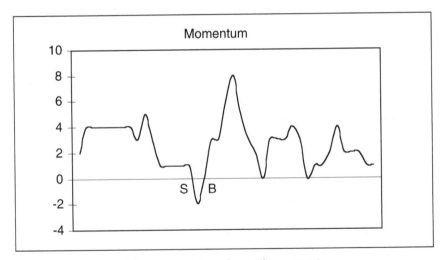

Figure 2.19 Resulting momentum from Figure 2.18

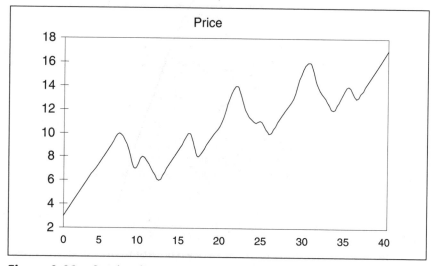

Figure 2.20   Stock price movement

suggests an overbought market and the stock price is expected to decrease. If D is below 20, this suggests an oversold market and the stock price is expected to increase. In Figure 2.21 the indicator D works well. After high levels of D, the stock price in Figure 2.20

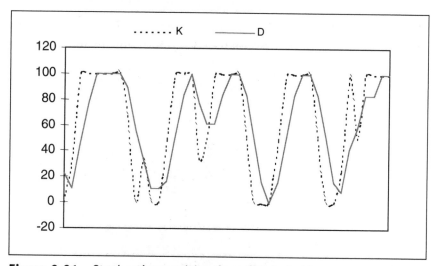

Figure 2.21   Stochastics resulting from Figure 2.20

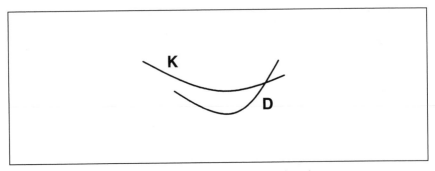

Figure 2.22   Crucial buy signal

decreases; after low levels of D, the stock price in Figure 2.20 increases.

The way in which K crosses D is also important. If at the crossing, K and D are both upward sloping, the buy signal is more crucial, as in Figure 2.22. If K is upward sloping, while D is still downward sloping, the buy signal is less crucial, as in Figure 2.23.

The same logic applies for a sell signal. If K and D are both downward sloping, the sell signal is more crucial.

Critical Appraisal of Technical Analysis

The underlying assumption of technical analysis that fundamental data are implicitly included in chart formations appears

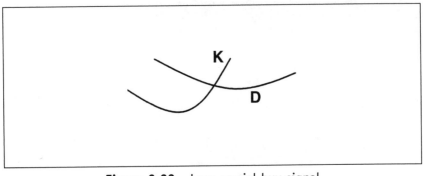

Figure 2.23   Less crucial buy signal

somewhat unrealistic and presumptuous. However, the psychological foundation of technical analysis is warranted in a financial market, where psychological factors weigh heavily. Therefore, a combination of fundamental analysis and technical analysis promises to yield the best trading results. Maybe future analysts will combine fundamental analysis and technical analysis in a coherent way.

Whatever critics say about technical analysis though, they can not ignore the "self fulfilling prophecy" factor: Because more and more traders use technical analysis and computer programs give buy and sell signals based on that theory, the market does move according to the principles of technical analysis. Therefore, no trader can afford to disregard it.

TIME SERIES ANALYSIS

Another way to predict stock prices is *time series analysis*. Time series analysis is the process of forecasting a stock price using statistical methods to analyze historical stock price time series.

The most common method used in time series analysis is *regression analysis*. In a regression analysis, the movement of the dependent variable (e.g., sales) is being explained by an independent variable (e.g., advertising). The difference between regression analysis and time series analysis is that in time series analysis the independent variable is simply time.

The easiest type of regression analysis is *linear* regression analysis. In a linear regression, a straight trend line (regression function) is derived and can then be extrapolated to forecast the movement of the stock. However, the linear regression analysis only gives good results if the source data itself behaves linearly.

If the source data is nonlinear, as in Figure 2.24, we have two options: Either try to fit the non-linear source data into a non-linear regression analysis, or transform the non-linear data into linear data and then perform a simple linear regression analysis.

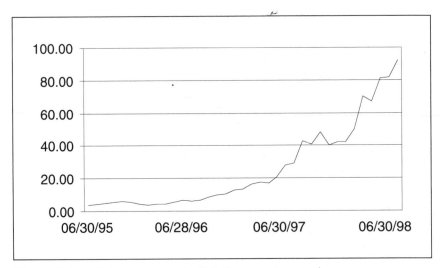

Figure 2.24   Price movement of Dell computer stock

Here we will choose the second option, which requires three steps:

1. Transform the non-linear data into linear data by taking the logarithm of the source data.
2. Perform the simple linear regression analysis.
3. De-logarithmatize the data and derive the non-linear regression function, which can be easily extrapolated to do the forecast.

Figure 2.24 shows the three-year price movement of the Dell computer stock price. As we can see, Dell increases exponentially. Figure 2.25 shows the natural logarithm of Figure 2.24. Since the logarithm of Dell stock in Figure 2.25 moves linearly on average, it follows that a linear regression analysis is appropriate to derive the average growth rate.

Let's now perform the standard linear regression analysis. We have to derive the regression function:

$$y = a + b\,t$$

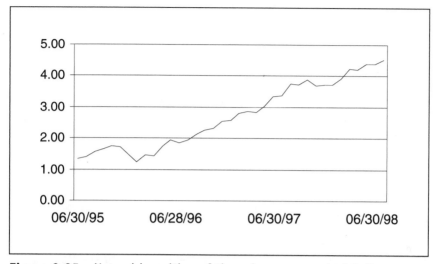

Figure 2.25 Natural logarithm of the price movement of Dell computer stock

where
  y = price of Dell stock
  a = value of y at t_0
  b = slope of y
  t = points in time
b and a can be calculated:

$$b = \frac{\frac{1}{n}\sum ty - \bar{t}\bar{y}}{\frac{1}{n}\sum t^2 - \bar{t}^2} \text{ and } a = \bar{y} - b\bar{t}$$

where $\bar{t}$ and $\bar{y}$ are the mean of t and y, respectively.

For time t we have end-of-month data for three years. Thus, we have the values 1, 2, 3, 4 … 36 for the time t. Using the data from Figure 2.25 we get b = 0.0978 and a = 0.9547. This results in the regression function r as shown in Figure 2.26.

To forecast the exponential Dell stock price movement, we now have to transform the parameters a and b from the linear regres-

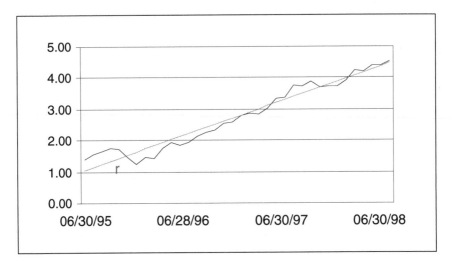

Figure 2.26 Regression function r of the logarithm of the Dell computer stock price

sion into the appropriate a_1 and b_1 of an exponential regression. A good approximation of the Dell price in Figure 2.24 is:

$$y = a_1 \times e^{\,b_1 t}$$

where e (Euler's constant) = 2.7182...,

Now, we can simply use $a_1 = e^a$, and $b = b_1$. Thus $a_1 = e^{0.9547} = 2.5978$ and $b_1 = 0.0978$.

Using these values for a_1 and b_1 with the original (non-logarithmic) Dell prices y at times t, we get the exponential regression function r_1 as shown in Figure 2.27.

We have now derived an exponential regression function, which reflects the trend of the stock price movement. This function can be used to forecast the Dell stock prices. The regression analysis derived a price of $2.5978 \times e^{(0.0978 \times 36)} = 87.84$ for June 30, 1998. (The number 36 represents 36 months in time, from July 31, 1995 to June 30, 1998.) The exponential regression analysis forecasts for December 31, 1998 (42 months) a Dell price of $2.5978 \times e^{(0.0978 \times 42)} = 157.95$. The reader, who is reading this book after December 31, 1998, can check the accuracy of this exponential trend forecast.

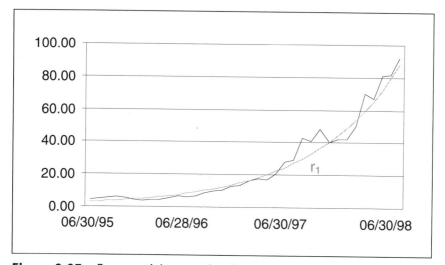

Figure 2.27 Exponential regression function r_1 of the Dell computer stock price

Overall, regression analysis is useful, but it is not an overly popular forecasting method. The reason is that it is non-causal, meaning it has only time as an explaining factor for the stock price movement.

It should be mentioned that exponentially smoothed moving averages, trend predictions such as the RSI, as well as momentum and stochastics can also be considered time series analysis. However as in this book, they are usually categorized within technical analysis.

FURTHER METHODS TO PREDICT STOCK PRICES

Econometric Models

Econometrics is a methodology that tests certain economic hypotheses with the help of mathematical-statistical systems of equations. Econometric models can have several hundred interdependent equations and variables. The equations are solved with the help of computers.

Econometric models can also try to predict stock price movements in an economy. A complex system of economic inputs of (presumably) all relevant economic data such as GDP growth, earnings expectation, unemployment data, current account balance, and much more leads to the forecast of stock price.

Econometrics, although very popular in the 1960s and 1970s, has lost scientific acceptance. In the recent past econometric models, such as the famous one by Elaine Garzarelli, have not predicted stock price movements very well. Questionable is the general concept of trying to capture the highly complex, psychologically based economic behavior of market participants in a series of mathematical equations.

Markov Process

A stochastic process describes the uncertain course that a variable, e.g., a stock price, follows through time. A *Markov process* is a specific type of stochastic process. The main characteristic of the Markov process is that it assumes all the relevant information to predict the future stock price movement is contained in the present stock price. Past data is principally irrelevant, especially the pattern in which the present stock price has emerged. Thus, the Markov process denies the basic principle of technical analysis, which says that the historical pattern of a stock price is the key to predicting the future stock price!

The Markov process does use past data though, especially the historical stock price volatility, in order to anticipate expected volatility. The Markov process also needs the expected return (price change + dividends) of a stock. The expected return is often derived on the basis of past returns.

The expected volatility and the expected return are used in a specific type of Markov process, the *Wiener process*. The Wiener process is often used to describe and forecast stock prices.

A generalized form of the Wiener process is:

$$\frac{\Delta S}{S} = \mu \times \Delta t + \sigma \times \Delta z$$

where

S = stock price

ΔS = change in the stock price

μ = expected stock return (price change + dividends)

Δt = period of time

σ = expected volatility

Δz = Wiener process, $\Delta z = \varepsilon\sqrt{\Delta t}$ where ε = random drawing from a standardized normal distribution (which has a mean of 0, and a variance of 1)

The left-hand side of the equation, ΔS/S, is the relative or percentage change of the stock price. For example, if the stock price has increased from 100 to 110, the change ΔS is 10. Thus ΔS/S = 10/100 or 10%. μ × Δt is the expected value of the return at time Δt. σ × Δz is the stochastic (unknown) part of the relative change of S.

Let's look at a generalized Wiener process in an example:

EXAMPLE 2.3

The present stock price is $150, next year's expected return is 20%, the annual expected volatility is 30%. The sample drawing from a standardized normal distribution results in + 1.

What is the stock price in one day (=1/365) due to the generalized form of the Wiener process?

Following the Wiener equation, the one-day change of the stock is:

$$\Delta S = 150 \times [(0.2 \times 1/365) + 0.3 \times 1 \times \sqrt{1/365}] = 2.44$$

Thus, the stock price after one day is assumed to be 150 + 2.44 = 152.44

Because the stock price prediction is partly determined by a random drawing from a normal distribution, this prediction methodology is called a *random walk* process. If a price follows a random walk process, this means that due to the random nature of the process, no successful trading strategy can be formulated. Thus, for anyone who believes in the random walk, this book is a complete waste of time.

Monte Carlo Simulation

Monte Carlo simulation is not a complete methodology on its own. It refers to any repeated simulation that randomly generates values, whereby the simulations are independent from each other. The term Monte Carlo is related to the casinos in Monte Carlo, where each gamble can be considered an independent simulation. Whatever number has been previously derived at a roulette table has no influence on the next gamble. Together with the binomial model, Monte Carlo simulation can be used to describe stock price behavior.

Monte Carlo Simulation in Combination with the Binomial Model
Let's assume a stock price follows a *binomial model*. The name binomial model stems from the fact that the stock can go two (bi) ways, up or down, within a certain time frame. As shown in Figure 2.28, if the stock is at $100 today, it can go higher or lower after a certain time period.

A four-step binomial model looks like the illustration in Figure 2.29. "u" denotes the degree of the upward move, "d" denotes the degree of the downward move. An upward move occurs with the probability p, and downward move occurs with the probability 1-p.

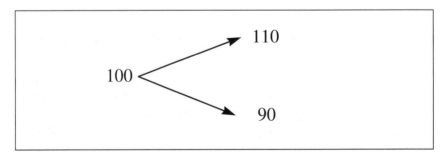

Figure 2.28   Possible movement of a stock in a one-step binomial model

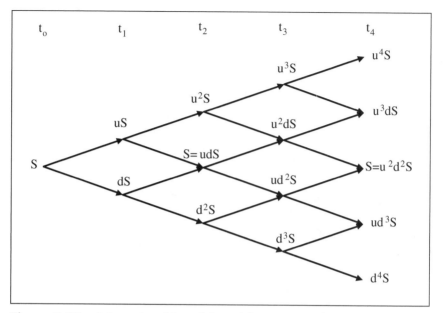

Figure 2.29 A four-step binomial model

EXAMPLE 2.4

The current price of a stock is S = $100, the yearly volatility is σ = 10%, each time step Δt = 1 year, the 1-year interest rate r = 5%, and the yearly dividend of the stock is q = 4.5%. What are the possible stock prices in a four-step binomial model after 4 years?

Using the formulas of the binomial model $u = e^{\sigma\sqrt{\Delta t}}$, we get u = 2.7183^{0.1 × 1} = 1.1052. d = 1/u = 1/1.1052 = 0.9048. The probability p = (e^{(r-q)\Delta t} - d)/(u - d), thus p = (2.7183^{(0.05-0.045) × 1} - 0.9048)/(1.1052 - 0.9045) = 0.5000 or 50%.

From Figure 2.30 we see that the possible stock prices after four years are 149.18, 122.14, 100, 81.87, and 67.03.

We can now use the Monte Carlo simulation to generate *one* likely stock price in four years. We randomly simulate each possible path through the tree.

As above, let's use "u" for an upward movement and "d" for a downward movement in the binomial tree. There is only one possi-

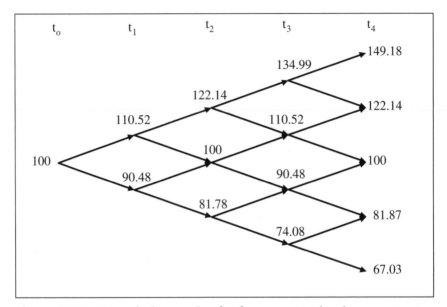

Figure 2.30   Numerical example of a four-step stock price movement

ble path that leads to price 149.18, which is going straight up, or uuuu. There are four possible paths that lead to the price 122.14: uuud, uudu, uduu, duuu; four possible paths to the price 100: uudd, udud, dduu, dudu; four possible paths to the price 81.87: dddu, ddud, dudd, uddd; and one path to the price 67.03, straight down, or dddd.

Table 2.1 shows the results of the Monte Carlo simulation of random paths through the tree in Figure 2.30: After each simulation the resulting price is stored. After all prices are generated, their average is calculated.

In our example, the probability of moving up is the same as the probability of moving down, 0.5. Also, there is one possible path to price 149.18 and one possible path to price 67.03. There are four possible paths to the prices 122.14, 100, and 81.87. Thus, altogether we have 14 possible paths. It follows that the Monte Carlo simulation should have come out to $1/14 \times 149.18 + 4/14 \times 122.14 + 4/14 \times 100 + 4/14 \times 81.87 + 1/14 \times 67.03 = 102.30$. We can see that

TABLE 2.1 Stock prices from the Monte Carlo
Simulation of Figure 2.30

Number of Simulations	Stock Price
10	106.85
100	100.92
1000	101.91
10000	102.27

the more simulations we do, the closer the Monte Carlo simulation
is approaching that result.

Neural Networks

A fairly new and increasingly popular methodology used to forecast
stock patterns and stock prices is Neural Networks. Neural Networks are designed to mimic the functioning of the human brain.
The name neural comes from *neuron,* a basic element of the human
brain. A neuron receives information, processes it, and carries out
a signal if a certain threshold is exceeded. For example, neurons
might receive information about cars approaching. If a certain car
gets closer than a certain threshold distance, an output signal, a
warning, is transmitted.

A sample structure of a neural network is shown in Figure 2.31.

With regard to stock forecasting, the input variables in Figure
2.31 might be fundamental data such as the price earnings ratio,
the return on equity, the dividend yield, or the earnings growth
rate. Also, technical data such as the MACD, RSI, Momentum, or
Stochastics (described earlier in this chapter) can serve as inputs.
Because Neural Networks are good at pattern recognition, graphical data such as resistance and support levels, double tops, head
and shoulder formations, and Elliot waves also can be used as
inputs.

In the hidden layer or layers the input variables are activated
and transformed. It is a widespread misconception that the struc-

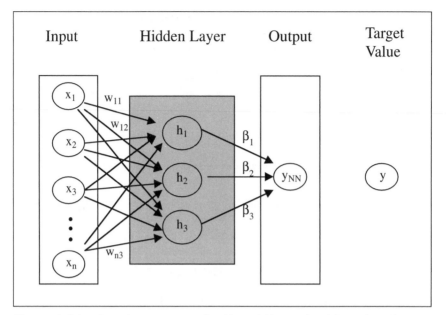

Figure 2.31   Sample structure of a Neural Network with various input variables x_i, $i = 1 \ldots n$, one hidden layer with three nodes h_j, $j = 1 \ldots 3$, and one output variable, y_{NN}

ture of the hidden layers is unknown. In most Neural Networks the mathematical algorithms of the hidden layers are clearly expressed and mostly differentiable.

In Figure 2.31 the output variable can be the model's stock price. This price is compared to the target value, which is the true stock price. One key feature of Neural Networks is that—like the human brain—that they are capable of *learning*. The process of learning is implemented with weighting factors. Each weighting factor has a resistance attached to it. Numerous simulations of different combinations of weighting factors are run. If the Neural Network output is close to the target value, the weighting factors are strengthened, i.e., the resistance is turned down. If certain weighting factors produce bad results, the weighting factors are weakened, i.e., the resistance is turned up. This recursive process of incrementally adjusting the weighting factors to approach a target value is called *backpropagation*.

Mathematically, a simple Neural Network process can be expressed as:

$$y_{NN} = \sum_{h=1}^{H} \beta_h \times T \sum_{i=1}^{n} w_{ih} x_i$$

where

y_{NN} = Output of the Neural Network (e.g., the price of a certain stock)

β_h = Weighting factor of layer node h_j, which reflects the strength between h_j and the output y_{NN} (see Figure 2.31)

T = Transfer function, usually a simple hyperbolic function such as the tangent function. This function standardizes weighted input variables to values between -1 and $+1$.

w_{ih} = Weighting factor of input x_i, which reflects the strength between input x_i and the hidden layer node h (see Figure 2.31)

x_i = Input variable i, (e.g., price earnings ratio or dividend yield)

In practice, Neural Networks are not developed enough to precisely predict a stock price. Rather, Neural Network models try to anticipate price patterns (Kamijo and Tanigawa, 1990), categorize stocks based on their performance (Yoon and Swales, 1991), determine optimal buy and sell signals (Kimoto, Asakawa, Yoda, and Takeoka; 1990), or predict the direction of stock movements (Kryzanowski, Galler, and Wright; 1993). Considering the progress in Neural Network analysis and increasing computer power, Neural Networks should become a major force in stock pattern and stock price predictions.

Neural Network models can also be built to closely resemble time series analysis. In this area, the advantage of Neural Networks is that they are able to input many variables and process them simultaneously. One disadvantage of Neural Networks is that they have few explanatory abilities. The result is measured strictly in terms of success predictability or failure. Seldom do Neural Networks contribute to the theoretical analysis.

Neural Networks Enhanced with Fuzzy Logic   A fuzzy logic system deals with imprecise terms such as: fairly strong buy signal, strong buy signal, very strong buy signal; maybe a trend, possibly a trend, probably a trend, or most certainly a trend. This is in contrast to traditional programming languages, which contain strict true/false and either/or statements.

Fuzzy logic tries to quantify these vague inputs and attempts to process them to support human decision making (e.g., an investment decision). Today fuzzy logic is used to run the Tokyo subway and other subway systems around the world (to implement longer stops during rush hours), in household appliances (to implement many different degrees of cooling for an air conditioner), electronic devices, and portfolio management.

Let's look at a fuzzy logic example: An investor will buy IBM, if fundamental analysis *or* technical analysis gives at least a "fairly strong" buy signal.

Fuzzy rule a) for fundamental analysis is:

If PE ratio = 90% → buy signal

AND revenue growth = 80% → buy signal

THEN possibly price increase of IBM

Fuzzy rule b) for technical analysis is:

If the technical indicator MACD = 40% → buy signal

AND RSI = 50% → buy signal

THEN possibly price increase of IBM

Since the fuzzy rules are combined with an AND statement, we take the minimum of the results:

Rule a): min(90%,80%) = 80%

Rule b): min(40%,50%) = 40%

Because the investor wants to buy if fundamental *or* technical analysis gives a buy signal, we take the maximum of the two rules:

Max(80%,40%) = 80%.

The fuzzy logic system returns an 80% buy signal, which the investor considers strong. He buys IBM.

Fuzzy logic can enhance Neural Networks. One of the main problems with Neural Networks is the amount of time it takes for the system to learn. Implementing fuzzy logic "if – then" rules can structure the hidden layers of Neural Networks. This can determine causal relationships between input variables and output data. If the relationship between certain input variables (e.g., earnings growth) and the output (e.g., upward trend of the price of IBM) is strong, the weighting factors of these input variables are prioritized and optimized. Thus, the backpropagation process can be done more quickly and effectively. Also, when integrating fuzzy logic into Neural Networks, the contribution to the theoretical analysis can be improved.

Chaos Theory

Chaos breeds life, whereas order breeds habit.
—Henry Adams

A *chaotic system* is a system that appears random, but has some hidden deterministic order. A chaotic system also exhibits a high sensitive dependence on initial conditions. This dependence was explained by Edward Lorenz (1972) with the popular "butterfly effect." Lorenz, a meteorologist at MIT, was testing weather forecasts with a nonlinear chaotic computer model. He found that only very small changes in the initial conditions lead to very big changes in the weather forecast. He explained the phenomenon by saying that "the flap of a butterfly's wings in Brazil could alter the weather in the United States," due to the chain reaction of turbulences caused by the Brazilian butterfly.

The search for an underlying order in a seemingly chaotic system is accomplished by looking at patterns. *Fractals* can help find these patterns.

First, let's categorize geometric objects: A point has the dimension zero, a line has one dimension, a surface has two dimensions, and all other objects (e.g., a dice, a butterfly) have three dimensions. Fractals are figures that have a non-integer dimension, in other words, they have a dimension in-between the defined dimensions. How can that be? Imagine you squeeze a cotton ball with a press as tightly as possible. Will the cotton ball now have only two dimensions? Neither it can be considered as having a dimension somewhere between two and three dimensions. The same logic applies to a straight line (one-dimensional), which is squeezed together to become a wiggly line. It can be considered to have a dimension in between one and two dimensions.

Mandelbrot (1983) has explained fractals with his famous paradigm which asks, "How long is the coast of Britain?" Measuring Britain's coastline with a 1-yard measuring stick will give a certain result. Measuring Britain's coast line with a 1-foot measuring stick will give a different, higher result, because more edges and corners of Britain's wiggly coastline will be captured. A smaller, 1-centimeter measuring stick will give an even higher result. Continuing this line of thought, the question arises: Is Britain's coastline (or that of any country) infinitely long?

Another property of fractals is their *self-similarity*. When magnifying or reducing a fractal object, the original object and the altered object show similarities. For example, the coastline of Britain viewed from 10,000 feet has similar structures and patterns when viewed from 10 feet. The branches of a tree close to the trunk have a structure similar to the smaller branches at the outer layers of the tree. The same logic may apply to time series:

A yearly price pattern that is observed with daily closing prices may have similarities to a daily pattern that is observed using every trading price.

Chaos Theory and the Financial Markets   The principle of chaos theory, to find a hidden order in a seemingly random time series, (e.g. a stock price series) naturally has a high appeal to stock market investors. In recent years, numerous studies have attempted to find a predictive value within chaos theory.

Brock, Hsieh, and LeBaron (1991) used features of chaos theory to divide time series into random, chaotic, or correlated. If the correlation dimension (the complexity of the system) remains roughly equal to its embedding dimension (the dimension of the phase space), a time series is considered random (see the previous section on the Markov process). In this case, a prediction of future prices is impossible due to the random nature of the process.

If the correlation dimension saturates with increasing embedding dimensions, the time series is considered chaotic. In this case short-term predictions are possible, but long-term predictions are impossible. This can be explained by the chaotic weather system: A weather forecast for 6, 12 or even 24 hours into the future is fairly reliable. A forecast for 48 hours into the future is less reliable. Due to the complex nature of the chaotic weather system, the longer the time horizon, the more difficult the prediction. After reaching a certain time horizon, e.g., 5 days, the system turns into chaos. In other words, due to its complex nature, it is not reliably predictable anymore.

Embrechts, Cader, and Deboeck (1994) derive that the Federal Funds rate followed a chaotic process during 1975 to 1991, but not during 1988 to 1991. In the latter period, the Fed Funds rate showed long-term predictability. U.S. Treasury notes tend to follow a biased random walk, whereas in the Swiss Frank/U.S. dollar market, long-term predictions are possible. The Japanese stock market seems to follow a random walk. Embrechts and others conclude that in some cases there is clear evidence of chaos, which allows only short-term predictions.

Numerous other studies (e.g., Larrain, 1991; Hsieh, 1991; Willey, 1992; Deboeck, 1994; Olson, 1998; Gwilym, 1999) have investigated whether stock-, bond-, commodity-, or currency prices follow a non-linear, chaotic process. Most researches have found at least some chaotic components within the financial time series and are in agreement that chaos theory is a helpful tool for better understanding the complex nature of the financial markets.

SUMMARY

This chapter outlined the contemporary methods for stock forecasting. The two main methods for stock forecasting today are fundamental analysis and technical analysis.

There are four basic components in fundamental analysis:

The political stability of the country to be invested in should be guaranteed.

The macro-economic situation, mainly comprised of the inflation rate, the gross domestic product (GDP), current account balance, and unemployment rate should underlie the investment decision.

Also sector specific data, especially the growth potential of the sector, should be a fundamental consideration when investing.

Naturally, the company's ratios, such as price earnings ratio, earnings per a share, return on equity, dividend yield, debt-equity, net working capital ratio, cash flow ratio, operating profit margin, and others are important fundamental investment criteria.

Technical analysis tries to forecast prices using the pattern the price has followed in the past. Technical analysis consists of many different methods, which are principally unrelated to each other. Among the most popular methods is the derivation of simple chart patterns such as resistance and support levels, double tops and bottoms, head and shoulder formation, and flags. Among the most popular theories are the Moving Average Convergence/Divergence (MACD), Fibonacci Ratios and Elliot Wave Principle, the Relative Strength Index (RSI), the Momentum analysis, and the Stochastics analysis.

Technical analysis is based on three crucial assumptions:

1. Chart patterns reflect the fundamental data in an economy or a company.
2. Markets move in trends.
3. History repeats itself.

Whereas assumptions 2 and 3 appear realistic, assumption 1 is one of the most criticized features of technical analysis. It follows that hard-line technical analysts are not interested in fundamental data itself.

Due to its heuristic (non-mathematical) nature, technical analysis can hardly be proven theoretically. In addition, technical analysis is difficult to prove empirically, due to its highly subjective nature.

Despite these drawbacks, the advantage of technical analysis is its simplicity. Chart patterns such as support and resistance levels, double tops, double bottoms, and flags can be spotted fast and without computation or calculation. The main justification of technical analysis lies in the field of psychology, namely self-fulfilling prophecy. Due to the fact that more and more traders use technical analysis, and computer programs give buy and sell signals based on that theory, the market does move according to the principles of technical analysis. A coherent theory that combines fundamental and technical analysis is yet to be found.

A popular method of predicting stock prices is a simple time series analysis. In a time series analysis the nature of the time series is detected. Then an extrapolation of the time series is done to predict the stock price in the future. The advantage of time series analysis is its simplicity. The drawback is that no causal relationship of the stock price and its determinants is established.

Other methods that try to forecast financial prices are:

- Econometric models, which try to forecast prices using a complex set of up to several hundred equations and variables. Naturally, computer power is used to solve the equations.

- The Markov process generates prices with the help of a random drawing from a standardized normal distribution. Due to the random nature of this stochastic process, reliable stock forecasting is assumed to be impossible.

- Neural Networks try to mimic the functioning of the human brain. Neural networks are capable of learning due to weighting factors that are strengthened when a good forecast is generated, and weakened when a bad forecast is generated. Neural Networks can be enhanced with fuzzy logic, a methodology that tries to quantify and structure vague input information.

- Chaos theory deals with systems that appear random, but have some hidden deterministic order. Chaotic systems show a high sensitivity to initial conditions. Numerous studies have tried to relate stock price behavior to chaos theory. If a given financial system is considered chaotic, only short-term predictions are possible. After a certain threshold is passed, the system becomes chaotic and therefore unpredictable.

SUGGESTED READING

Achelis, S., (1995). *Technical Analysis from A to Z,* (New York: Probus Publishing Co.).

Brock, W., D. Hsieh, and B. LeBaron, (1991). "Nonlinear Dynamics, Chaos, and Instability: Statistical Theory and Economic Evidence," (Cambridge, MA: The MIT Press).

Copsey, I., (1993). "The Principles of Technical Analysis," (Chicago: Dow Jones Telerate).

Deboeck, G., editor, (1994). *Trading on the Edge, Neural, Genetic, and Fuzzy Systems for Chaotic Financial Markets,* (New York: John Wiley & Sons).

Dorsey, Thomas J., (1995). *Point and Figure Charting: The Essential Application for Forecasting and Tracking Market Prices,* (New York: John Wiley and Sons, Inc.).

Edwards, Robert Davis, (1992). "Technical Analysis of Stock Trends," (Boston, MA.: John Magee; New York: Distributed by New York Institute of Finance, Business Information & Publishing).

Embrechts, M., M. Cader, and G. Deboeck, (1994). "Nonlinear Dimensions of Foreign Exchange, Stock, and Bond Markets" in Deboeck, G., Editor, *Trading on the Edge, Neural, Genetic, and Fuzzy Systems for Chaotic Financial Markets,* (New York: John Wiley & Sons).

Fischer, Robert, (1993). *Fibonacci Applications and Strategies for Traders,* (New York: John Wiley and Sons).

Gwilym, O., C. Brooks, A. Claire, and S. Thomas, (1999). "Tests on Nonlinearity Using LIFFE Futures Transactions Price Data", in *Manchester School,* 67(2), pp. 167–186.

Hexton, Richard, (1993). *Technical Analysis in the Options Markets: The Effective Use of Computerized Trading Systems,* (London: Kogan Page).

Hsieh, D. A. (1991). "Chaos and Nonlinear Dynamics: Application to Financial Markets," *Journal of Finance 46* (5), pp. 1839–1877.

Kamijo, K., and T., Tanagawa, (1990). "Stock Price Pattern Recognition. A Recurrent Neural Network Approach." in *Proceedings of the Second International Joint Conference on Neural Networks,* (San Diego).

Kimoto, T., K. Asakawa, M. Yoda, and M. Takeoka, (1990). "Stock Market Prediciton System with Modular Neural Networks." in *Proceedings of the International Joint Conference of Neural Networks,* (San Diego).

Kryzanowski, L., M. Galler, and D. W. Wright, (1993). "Using Artificial Neural Networks to Pick Stocks," Financial Analysts Journal, July–August, pp. 21–27.

Larrain, M., (1991). "Testing Chaos and Nonlinear Dynamics in T-Bill Rates," *Financial Analysts Journal,* September–October, pp. 51–62.

Meissner, G., (1998). *Trading Financial Derivatives, Futures, Swaps and Options in Theory and Application,* (New York: Simon and Schuster).

Olson, R., (1998). "Behavioral Finance and Its Implications for Stock-price Volatility," *Financial Analysts Journal,* 54(2): 10–18.

Refenes, A., editor, (1995). *Neural Networks in the Capital Markets,* (New York: John Wiley & Sons).

Trippi, R., (1995). *Chaos and Nonlinear Dynamics in the Financial Markets: Theory, Evidence, and Applications,* (Burr Ridge, IL: Irwin Professional Publishing).

Trippi, R., and Jae Lee, (1996). *Artificial Intelligence in Financing and Investing,* (Chicago: Irwin Professional Publishing).

White, H., (1993). "Economic Prediction Using Neural Networks: The Case of IBM Daily Stock Prices." Proceedings of the IEEE International Conference on Neural Networks, July 1988, pp. II–451–58. Reprinted from *Neural Networks in Finance and Investing,* (Chicago: Probus Publishing Co.).

Willey, T., (1992). "Testing for Nonlinear Dependence in Daily Stock Indexes," *Journal of Economics and Business* 44(1), 63–76.

Yoon, Y., and G. Swales, (1991). "Predicting Stock Price Performance: A Neural Network Approach." Proceedings of the Twenty-fourth Annual Hawaii International Conference of Systems Sciences, Hawaii, *IEEE Computer Society Press,* 4, pp. 156–162.

3

OUTPERFORMING THE DOW USING PORTFOLIO STRATEGIES

Tactics are for speculators, strategies for investors.

This chapter shows various methods of selecting stock portfolios that have significantly outperformed the Dow in the past. All methods are easy to use and can be applied by the reader.

INTRODUCTION

When selecting stock portfolios and testing their historical performance, the first question that arises is how much historical data should be tested. The authors of this book have agreed to use data from last the 15 years for the portfolio testing. Testing the portfolio strategies for longer and shorter durations yields slightly different results, but the principles remain the same.

Because stocks in the Dow are replaced periodically (as described in Chapter 1), we included 42 stocks in the study. The stocks had to be re-adjusted for stock splits. Dividends are part of the return of a stock and are therefore included in the study. The effect of taxes and commissions are omitted.

Each portfolio strategy is implemented for one year. After one year, the results of the selected portfolios are tested. The authors chose July 1 of each year to implement and check each portfolio's performance, in order to eliminate year-end fluctuations.

THE PORTFOLIO STRATEGIES

In the following section, we will describe the three portfolio strategies that were tested and that significantly outperformed the Dow.

- Last Year's Winners
- Fool's Four
- Smooth Risers

Last Year's Winners

The "Last Year's winners" portfolio strategy is based on long-term trends in the stock market. The strategy proclaims that a stock which has outperformed the market will continue its upward momentum and will rise more than the market average. The Last Year's Winners strategy is very simple. It consists of a portfolio made up of the top five performing stocks during the previous twelve months, based on percentage increase of return (the percentage growth plus the dividend).

The selection process occurs once a year. As mentioned, the authors chose July 1 as a selection date to eliminate year-end distortions.

Fool's Four

The "Fool's Four" has been a successful strategy since it was popularized by Michael O'Higgins and John Downes in their 1991 book,

Beating the Dow. It is now the centerpiece of the "Motley Fool Investment Guide" Internet site and the best selling investing guide by the same name from brothers David and Tom Gardner (1996).

The Fool's Four works as follows:

1. The ten highest yielding stocks (dividend divided by stock price) of the Dow in the last twelve months are selected.
2. Of those ten stocks, the five with the lowest price are selected.
3. Of those five stocks, the one with the lowest price is omitted.
4. The stock with the second lowest price gets a weighting of 40%. The other three stocks get a weighting of 20% each.

For example, let's assume the five cheapest stocks of the ten highest yielding stocks are International Paper, General Motors, Chevron, 3M, and General Electric. If International Paper is the one with the lowest price, we disregard it. If we plan to invest $5,000 and General Motors is the second cheapest, $2,000 is invested in General Motors, and $1,000 apiece are invested in Chevron, 3M, and General Electric.

With the fool's four strategy, the investor will actually end up picking stocks that have under-performed the market. The reason is because, as already mentioned, companies try to moderately increase, or at least preserve their level of dividends. This being the case, the stocks with decreasing stock prices are the ones with the highest dividend yield (dividend yield = dividend divided by stock price). These are the stocks picked in the fool's four strategy.

The fool's four strategy assumes that it is these neglected under-performers that are the best buy (except for the worst one). The fool's four strategy believes in the long-term health of Dow stocks, i.e., that management will ultimately take the right action to bring the company back on track.

The good results of the fool's four strategy (see below) support this view. IBM, for example, suffered from what they called "brain drain" following their success in the 1960s and early 1970s. Older workers retired and younger ones were snatched up by the emerging competition. This left IBM with a less educated work force, which appeared detrimental to their future business prospects. A less widely held company might have failed altogether.

The fact that IBM was (and still is) one of the most widely held stocks in the world brought enormous pressure on the board of directors. They finally decided to take big risks, reorganized the company, shut down marginally profitable sectors, and ended the concept of lifetime employment. As a result, IBM recovered from a low of $23 per share in May 1995 to $120 per share in May 2000.

This same recovery has happened to other stocks in the Dow. Examples include American Telephone & Telegraph Inc., Goodyear Tire, Eastman Kodak, and Boeing. The resilience that the Dow companies tend to have because of their immense financial, legal, and human resources makes a portfolio of Dow stocks a low-risk investment.

Smooth Risers

The "Smooth Risers" strategy is based on the premise that a good performing stock rises in a very steady, non-volatile way. Therefore, the smooth risers are selected using volatility. Volatility measures the degree of relative fluctuation of a price. The higher the fluctuation, the higher the volatility and vice versa. For a detailed discussion on volatility, see Chapter 6.

The smooth risers strategy works as follows:

1. The ten best performing stocks of the last twelve months are selected from the Dow.
2. The five stocks with the lowest volatility are bought.

As with "Last Year's Winners" and "Fool's Four," the selection process is done once a year. Again, July 1, was the selection date.

USING PORTFOLIO STRATEGIES

In numerical terms, the result of the strategies relative to the Dow are summarized in Table 3.1.

From Table 3.1 we can see that all tested strategies outperformed the Dow significantly. Fool's Four comes in first with an average yearly gain of 23.6%. Last Year's Winner is second with 21.8% and the volatility-based Smooth Risers strategy is third with 19.1%.

When investing, not only the profit but also the *risk* is important. The risk is measured in terms of *volatility*. Volatility measures the relative fluctuation of a variable, in this case a certain strategy. A nice interpretation of volatility is "Investor Stress factor" which some newspapers use to express the risk involved. For a detailed analysis of volatility, see Chapter 6.

Table 3.2 shows the performance of the strategies together with the volatility.

From Table 3.2 we can see that the Dow actually had the lowest volatility, thus the lowest risk. This supports the assumption that higher profits come at the cost of higher risk.

Table 3.2 shows that the second best performing strategy, Last Year's Winners has the lowest volatility or risk of the three strategies. This raises the value of the Last Year's Winners strategy, which is supported by the fact that the Last Year's Winners portfolio only had one negative year during the period studied. Another point in favor of Last Year's Winners is that it is the easiest strategy to implement. The five best performing stocks are simply

TABLE 3.1 Results of the Three Strategies Relative to the Dow from 1973 to 1998

	Dow	Last Year's Winners	Fool's Four	Smooth Risers
Profit	15.1%	21.8%	23.6%	19.1%

TABLE 3.2 Performance and Risk of the Three Strategies from 1973 to 1998

	Dow	Last Year's Winners	Fool's Four	Smooth Risers
Profit	15.1%	21.8%	23.6%	19.1%
Volatility	11.5%	13.8%	25.5%	14.3%
Max. Profit in a Year	33.5%	36.9%	89.2%	42.7%
Min. Profit in a Year	−8.9%	−7.6%	−15.1%	−9.6%
Max.-Min. Diff.	42.4%	44.6%	104.3%	52.3%

selected and bought. The different methods of determining the five best stocks are as follows:

Method 1

Buy the five stocks that had the highest return in the previous 12 months (Last Year's Winners Strategy).

Table 3.2 shows that the Fool's Four strategy was the best performer of all strategies with an average annual return of 23.6%. However, this return carries the highest risk volatility of all strategies. Nevertheless, from it we derive Method 2:

Method 2

Of the ten highest yielding stocks, buy the second, third, fourth, and fifth cheapest. Weight the second cheapest with 40%, the others with 20% (Fool's Four Strategy).

Much of the overall success of the Fool's Four is dependent on one year's performance, in which Goodyear Tire Corp. experienced a 182% gain. If the individual stock appreciation gains are limited to 100% to eliminate extremes, the Fool's Four average performance drops to second place behind the Last Year's Winners with an average return of 21.8%.

Table 3.2 shows that the Smooth Risers strategy has an annual average return of 19.1%. It has a relatively low risk when compared to the other strategies. Thus, we obtain Method 3:

Method 3

Of the ten best performing stocks, buy the five with the lowest volatility (Smooth Risers Strategy).

As mentioned, with all strategies the authors applied July 1 as a rollover date. When testing the strategies for other rollover dates, the results were—as expected—slightly different numerically, but there was no change in the profit ranking of the strategies.

All strategies are based on their historical performance. While there is naturally no guarantee that past performance guarantees future performance, there is ample evidence of repetitive investor behavior. Therefore, the strategies should continue to outperform the Dow in the long run, but naturally, there is no guarantee that the strategies outperform the Dow each individual year.

SUMMARY

In this chapter, three distinct portfolio strategies were derived and tested. All portfolios have significantly outperformed the Dow in the past.

The Last Year's Winners strategy is the easiest to implement. Simply the five best performing stocks of last year are purchased and held for one year. This strategy has outperformed the Dow annually by 6.7% over the last 15 years. The Last Year's winners strategy has the lowest risk compared with other portfolio strategies.

In contrast to the Last Year's Winner's strategy, the Fool's Four strategy is based on stocks that have under-performed the market. Out of the ten highest yielding stocks, the five cheapest are bought.

The very cheapest is omitted, the second cheapest is weighted with 40%, and the other three stocks are assigned 20% each.

The Fool's Four strategy has outperformed the Dow by 8.5% annually over the last 15 years. This good performance comes at the cost of relatively high risk in comparison to the other portfolio strategies.

The Smooth Risers strategy is based on volatility: Out of the ten best performing stocks, the five with the lowest volatility are selected. The Smooth Risers strategy has outperformed the Dow by 4% annually over the last 15 years. It has a fairly low risk compared with the Last Year's Winners and the Fool's Four strategies.

All strategies in this chapter are based on past performance. While it can be expected that they will continue to outperform the Dow in the long run, there is no guarantee for their success over short periods of time.

SUGGESTED READING

Bary, A., (1998). "Bound for the Pound?," *Barrons,* 78(52), p. 16–17.

Gardner, D., and Tom Gardner, (1996). *The Motley Fool Investment Guide: How the fool beats Wall Street's wise men and how you can too,* (New York: Simon and Schuster).

Kadlec, D. (1997). "The Dogs of the Dow Won't Hunt," *Time,* 150(24), p. 76.

Lynch, P., and John Rotchild, (1989). *One Up on Wall Street: How to Use What You Know to Make Money in the Market,* (New York: Simon and Schuster).

O'Higgens, M., and John Downes, (1991). *Beating the Dow, A High Return, Low Risk Method for Investing in the Dow Jones Industrial Stocks with as Little as $5,000,* (New York: HarperCollins Publishers).

Sheimo, M., (1999). *Stock Market Rules,* (New York: McGraw-Hill).

Stillman R., (1986). *Dow Jones Industrial Average: History and Role in the Investment Strategy,* (Homewood, IL: Dow Jones-Irwin).

4

OUTPERFORMING THE DOW USING FUTURES

Cheer up! The worst is yet to come.

—Philander Johnson

Before we come up with several robust methods to beat the Dow Jones Industrial Average using futures, let's first look at the main features of futures.

FUTURES: AN INTRODUCTION

A *future* is the agreement between two parties to trade a certain asset, at a certain future date, at a price which is agreed upon today.

A futures transaction is a bet. The future buyer bets on an increasing underlying asset price; the future seller bets on a decreasing underlying asset price. More precisely, someone who buys a future today is betting that at future maturity, the underlying asset price will be higher than today's future price. The seller who sells a future today bets that at future maturity, the underlying asset price will be lower than today's future price.

The *underlying asset* of the bet, i.e., Gold for a Gold future contract, or the Dow Jones for the Dow Jones future contract, primarily determines the price of the future contract. Let's look at a typical future trade. In Example 4.1, the future buyer does not wait until the maturity date of the future, but sells his future contract before future maturity.

EXAMPLE 4.1

An investor believes that the Dow Jones Industrial Average will go up. On January 4, he buys one Dow Jones future contract (without paying a premium, see below) at the market price of 10,755. (He cannot buy the future at a different price.) The Dow future price does go up. On January 28, the Dow future has a market price of 10,835. The investor sells his future contract at 10,835. (He cannot sell the future at a different price.) Since one point in the Dow future equals $10, the investor made a profit of (10,835 – 10,755) × $10 = $800.

Had the Dow future decreased to 10,655, then the investor would have lost (10,655 – 10,755) × $10 = $1,000.

Futures can be categorized in four groups as shown in Figure 4.1.

THE MAIN FEATURES OF FUTURES

A futures contract is characterized by three important items:

1. The future price, which is the delivery price (the price at which the underlying asset will be delivered at future maturity).
2. Expiration dates (last trading day and delivery date).
3. Specification of the deliverable asset (i.e., contract size, maturity, issuer for interest rate futures, quality of the prod-

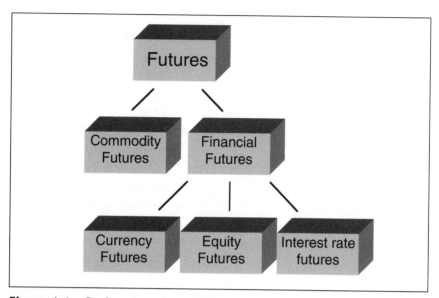

Figure 4.1 Basic categories of futures

uct for commodity futures, the composition of the index for index equity futures, etc.).

It is important to note that every future trade is executed at the current market future price. This future price is easily accessible on data services (CNBC, Bloomberg, Reuters, Telerate, etc). The future price is the price that is derived through supply and demand in the market. It is thus a *fair market future price* for the underlying asset with delivery at future maturity.

Therefore, the future buyer *does not pay a premium* to the future seller at the moment of the trade. (It's like buying a used car at the fair mid-market price with forward delivery. Neither the buyer nor the seller makes a profit from the deal.) Rather, the future buyer will pay the future price at future maturity and receive the underlying asset.

Futures are usually *not held until the maturity date*. As in example 4-1, a future trader can close his position at any time during the life of a future contract. Thus, the original future buyer can sell his future, and the original future seller can buy back his future contract. If a future buyer still holds the futures contract after the last trading day, the future buyer will have to buy the underlying asset at the delivery price. If a future seller still holds the futures contract after the last trading day, the future seller will have to sell the underlying asset at the delivery price.

As already discussed, the *delivery price* of an underlying asset is determined by the price at which the future trades at the time of the original future trade. So, if a trade of the 30-year Treasury future is executed at a price of $99 on January 13, then $99 will be the delivery price of the Treasury-bond when the future expires in March.

When trading a future, the distinction between *price* and *value* is important. In the above example, $99 is the future trading price and the delivery price of the Treasury bond. As already explained, every future deal is executed at that moment's fair market future price. Therefore, at the time the deal is done, the value of the trade is zero for the future buyer and the future seller. If the future moves up to 100, the value of the deal per one contract will be $(100 - 99) \times \$1,000 \times 1/100 = \$1,000$. That is, + $1,000 for the buyer of the future and − $1,000 for the seller.

There are several important dates regarding the *expiration* of futures. Futures are generally characterized by their *expiration months*. For U.S., European, and Asian interest rate futures, the expiration months are March, June, September, and December. Commodity futures expire more often, i.e., oil futures expire on a monthly basis.

The *last trading day* of a future is determined by the exchange. It is the last day a trader can offset his or her open position. An open position is an overall long or short position. If a trader had bought ten futures contracts, he or she can sell ten futures until the last trading day to offset the open position and reduce the trader's futures exposure to zero, and vice versa.

If a trader has a short futures position after the last trading day, he or she must deliver the underlying asset on the *delivery day*. Usually a first and a last notice day exist, which are the days on which an open position holder has to notify the exchange of the delivery.

For many commodity futures contracts however, delivery can take place during the whole expiration month of the futures contract. This gives the short futures holder an additional option.

Another feature of a futures contract is the *specification of the deliverable asset*. In a future contract, the issuer, maturity, and the contract size have to be specified. For example, the holder of a 30-year treasury future at the delivery date will receive a U.S. government bond, which matures 15 years or more from the delivery date. The principal amount of the bond has to be $100,000.

A seller of the 10-year German Bund future can deliver any German government bond with a maturity of 8.5 to 10 years. The principal amount is DM 250,000.

For an agricultural future, specifying the exact quality of the deliverable product is important. For the light sweet crude oil future for example, the New York Mercantile Exchange specifies the quality as: "Deliverable crude oil graded with 0.5% or less sulfur by weight, not less than 34° nor more than 45° API gravity. The following streams are available: West Texas Intermediate (WTI), Mid-Continent Sweet, Low Sweet Mix, New Mexican Sweet, North Texas Sweet, Oklahoma Sweet, South Texas Sweet, Brent Blend, Bonny Light, Oseberg, and Forties."

In the equity market, futures are traded on indexes. In the United States, the most widely traded stock index futures are the futures on the Dow, S&P 500, the Nasdaq 100, on the NYSE Composite index, on the Russell 2000, the S&P Mid-Cap 400, and on the Value Line Index.

TRADING FUTURES

Let's first discuss an important issue: Is trading futures free? The answer is: Pretty much. As mentioned above, the value of a futures trade at the time the trade is done is zero. Indeed, the buyer and the seller do not exchange money at that time. However, at the time of delivery, the buyer has to pay the futures price and will receive the underlying asset. Furthermore, the buyer and the seller of futures have to deposit insurance money because their futures trade can lead to a loss. This insurance money is called the *margin*.

The Margin System

The purpose of the margin system is to ensure that traders who lose money on their futures trades are able to pay their debt. The level of the margins is determined by the exchange. Broker companies can set the margins higher to increase the degree of insurance, but cannot set margins lower than those determined by the exchange.

There are basically three types of margins:

- the initial margin
- the maintenance margin
- the variation margin

The *initial margin* is, as expected, the margin that a buyer and a seller have to deposit when executing a future trade. The *maintenance margin* is lower than the initial margin. It is the lowest level to which the initial margin is allowed to drop. When losses have accumulated to more than the maintenance margin, the trader receives a margin call and is asked to deposit additional money, known as the *variation margin*. Depositing the variation margin brings the trader's account back to its initial margin. Therefore, the variation margin reflects the total amount lost by the trader. Example 4.2 and Table 4.1 show the functioning of the margin system.

EXAMPLE 4.2

A trader buys one crude oil futures contract at $25. The initial margin, set by the New York Mercantile Exchange, is $2,000. The maintenance margin is $1,500.

On days three and five, the margin account balance is lower than the required maintenance margin of $1,500. Therefore, a

TABLE 4.1 Margin Calls for a Long Position of One Crude Oil Futures Contract with an Initial Margin of $2,000 and a Maintenance Margin of $1,500

Day	Crude Oil Price	Profit/Loss	Cumulative Profit/Loss	Margin Account Balance	Variation Margin Call
1	25.00			2,000	
2	24.70	−300	−300	1,700	
3	23.90	−800	−1,100	900	1,100
4	23.90	0	−1,100	2,000	
5	22.50	−1,400	−2,500	600	1,400

margin call is triggered, and the future buyer has to bring the margin account balance back to the initial margin of $2,000.

On day five, the trader has lost $2,500, which equals the total amount of the variation margin.

If the crude oil futures had gone up, the trader would have been allowed to withdraw any amount of money in excess of $2000 from the margin account.

In reality, the initial margin and the maintenance margin vary strongly depending on the tick value (price movement value) and the volatility of a contract. Since the S&P future is a heavy contract, where a one-point move equals $250, the margins for buying or selling the S&P futures contracts are among the highest in the futures market. Although it varies from broker to broker, the initial margin can be as high as $24,000, and the maintenance margin is around $19,000 per futures contract. For lighter contracts, like the crude oil future in Example 4.2 above, margins are lower. The 30-treasury benchmark future has a one-point value of $1,000. However, because the contract is usually less volatile than a stock index futures contract, the margins are quite low. The initial margin is around $3,000, and the maintenance margin is around $2,000 per contract.

Some brokers pay interest on the margin accounts that exceed a certain amount, e.g., $100,000. The interest rate can be the 30-day T-bill offered rate, or similar actual market rates. If a trader is unable to deposit the variation margin, the broker closes the position. In Example 4.2, the broker would sell one futures contract.

Overall, the margin system of exchanges has worked fairly well. The inability to meet margin requirements, as in the case of Nick Leeson, who ruined Barings Bank in 1995 with excessive speculation, has been rare, however quite disastrous.

Let's look at the most popular future contracts. Table 4.2 shows the commodity future contracts traded on U.S. exchanges, which are divided into Metals, Energies, Grains & Legumes, Meats, and Exotics. Table 4.3 shows the financial futures on U.S. exchanges, which are categorized in currencies, interest rate, and indices.

Among the biggest exchanges in the U.S. are the AMEX (American Stock Exchange), CBOT (Chicago Board of Trade), CME (Chicago Mercantile Exchange), CBOE (Chicago Board of Option Exchange), the MA (Mid-America Commodity Exchange), NYMEX (New York Mercantile Exchange), and the NYSE (New York Stock Exchange).

The letters representing the expiry months (Column 5 in Tables 4.2 and 4.3) are F=January, G=February, H=March, J=April, K=May, M=June, N=July, Q=August, U=September, V=October, X=November, and Z=December.

Marking-to-Market

The daily process of calculating the profit/loss of every account on an exchange (as shown in Table 4.1) is called marking-to-market. Marking-to-market is easy when an asset is liquid. However, when an asset has not been trading for a while, it is not so easy to determine the mid-market price. This has led to manipulation of the mid-market price and the overstating of profits. As a result, independent determination of mid-market prices by a middle office of a company is necessary to prevent false profit reporting.

TABLE 4.2 Commodity Futures Contract Specification

COMMODITY FUTURES CONTRACT SPECIFICATIONS

Metals	Exch.	Hours (Ltd.)	Size	Months	Fluctuation	Pt. Value
Gold, KILO	CBOT	7:20–1:40	32.15 OZ	GJMQVZ	$.01/OZ = $3.215	$1.00 = $32.15
Gold, N.Y.	CMX	7:20–1:30	100 OZ	GJMQVZ	$.01/OZ = $10.00	$1.00 = $100
Gold, N.Y.	EFP	1:30PM–7:20AM	100 OZ	GJMQVZ	$.01/OZ = $10.00	$1.00 = $100
Copper	CMX	7:10–1:00	25,000 LBS	ALL	.05C/LB = $12.50	$.01 = $250
Palladium	NYMEX	7:10–1:20	100 OZ	HMUZ	$.05/OZ = $5.00	$1.00 = $100
Platinum	NYMEX	7:20–1:30	50 OZ	FJNV	$.01/OZ = $5.00	$1.00 = $50
Silver, N.Y.	CMX	7:25–1:25	5,000 OZ	HKNUZ	.10C/OZ = $5.00	$.01 = $50
Silver, N.Y.	EFP	1:25PM–7:25AM	5,000 OZ	HKNUZ	.10C/OZ = $5.00	$.01 = $50
Silver, New	CBOT	7:25–1:25	1,000 OZ	GJMQVZ	.10C/OZ = $1.00	$.01 = $10
Energies						
Crude Oil	NYMEX	8:45–2:10 (1:40–2:10)	1,000 BBL	ALL	$.01/BBL = $10.00	$1.00 = $1000
Heating Oil	NYMEX	8:50–2:10 (1:40–2:10)	42,000 GALS	ALL	0.01C/GAL = $4.20	$.01 = $420
Unleaded Gas	NYMEX	8:50–2:10 (1:40–2:10)	42,000 GALS	ALL	0.01C/GAL = $4.20	$.01 = $420
Natural Gas	NYMEX	9:00–2:10	10,000 MMBTU	ALL	.1C/MMBTU = $10.00	$.01 = $100
Electricity	NYMEX	8:55–2:30	736 MWH/MONTH	ALL	$.01/MWH = $7.36	
Grains & Legumes						
Corn	CBOT	9:30–1:15 (12:00)	5,000 BUSHELS	HKNUZ	1/4C/BU = $12.50	$.01 = $50
Corn	MA	9:30–1:45 (12:15)	1,000 BUSHELS	HKNUZ	1/8C/BU = $1.25	$.01 = $10
Oats	CBOT	9:30–1:15 (12:00)	5,000 BUSHELS	HKNUZ	1/4C/BU = $12.50	$.01 = $50
Oats	MA	9:30–1:45 (12:15)	1,000 BUSHELS	HKNUZ	1/8C = $1.25	$.01 = $10
Rice	CRCE	9:15–1:30	2,000 CWT (200,000 L)	FHKNUX	$.005/CWT = $10.00	$.01 = $20
Soybeans	CBOT	9:30–1:15 (12:00)	5,000 BUSHELS	FHKNUQX	1/4C = $12.50	$.01 = $50
Soybeans	MA	9:30–1:45 (12:15)	1,000 BUSHELS	FHKNUQX	1/8C = $1.25	$1.00 = $100

(Continued)

TABLE 4.2 (Continued)

COMMODITY FUTURES CONTRACT SPECIFICATIONS

Grains & Legumes

Soybeans Meal	CBOT	9:30–1:15 (12:00)	100 TONS	FHKNQUVZ	$.10/TON = $10.00	$1.00 = $20
Soybeans Meal	MA	9:30–1:45 (1:15)	50 TONS	FHKNQUVZ	$.10 = $2.00	$.01 = $600
Soybeans Oil	CBOT	9:30–1:15 (12:00)	60,000 LBS	FHKNQUVZ	$.0001/LB = $6.00	$.01 = $10
Soybeans Oil	MA	9:30–1:45	30,000 LBS	FHKNQUVZ	2.5/100LB = $6.25	$.01 = $50
Wheat	CBOT	9:30–1:15 (12:00)	5,000 BUSHELS	HKNUZ	1/4C/BU = $12.50	$.01 = $50
Wheat	KCBT	9:30–1:15	5,000 BUSHELS	HKNUZ	1/4C = $12.50	$.01 = $50
Wheat	MGE	9:30–1:15	5,000 BUSHELS	HKNUZ	1/4C = $12.50	$.01 = $50
Wheat	MA	9:30–1:45 (12:15)	1,000 BUSHELS	HKNUZ	1/8C = $1.25	$.01 = $10
Project A Grains	CBOT	10:30PM–4:30AM				

Meats

Feeder Cattle	CME	9:05–1:00 (12:00)	50,000 LBS	FHJKQUVX	2.5 POINTS = $12.50	$.01 = $500
Live Cattle	CME	9:05–1:00 (12:00)	40,000 LBS	GJMQVZ	2.5 POINTS = $10.0	$.01 = $400
Live Cattle	MA	9:05–1:15 (12:15)	20,000 LBS	GJMQVZ	2.5 POINTS = $5.00	$.01 = $200
Lean Hogs	CME	9:10–1:00 (12:00)	40,000 LBS	GJMNQVZ	2.5C/100LB = $10.00	$.01 = $400
Lean Hogs	MA	9:10–1:15 (12:15)	20,000 LBS	GJMNQVZ	2.5C/LB = $5.00	$.01 = $200
Pork Bellies	CME	9:10–1:00 (12:00)	40,000 LBS	GHKNQ	2.5C/100LB = $10.00	$.01 = $400

Exotics

Cocoa	CSCE	8:00–1:00	10 METRIC TONS	HKNUZ	1 POINT = $10.00	$1.00 = $10
Coffee	CSCE	8:15–12:32	37,500 LBS	HKNUZ	1 POINT = $3.75	$.01 = $375
Cotton	NYCE	9:30–1:40 (11:30)	50,000 LBS	ALL	.01C/LB = $5.00	3C/LB = $1,500
Orange Juice	NYCE	9:15–1:15 (11:00)	15,000 LBS	FHKNUX	.05C/LB = $7.50	$.01 = $150
Sugar	CSCE	8:30–12:20	112,000 LBS	HKNV	1 POINT = $11.20	$.01 = $1,120
Lumber	CME	9:00–1:05 (12:05)	80,000 LBS	FHKNUX	10C/1000 = $8.00	$.01 = $800

Source: First American Discount Corporation, reprinted with permission.

TABLE 4.3 Financial Futures Contract Specifications

FINANCIAL FUTURES CONTRACT SPECIFICATIONS

Currencies	Exch.	Hours (Ltd.)	Size	Months	Fluctuation	Pt. Value
Australian Dollar	CME	7:20–2:00 (9:16)	AD 100,000	HMUZ	1 PT = $10.00	1.00 = $1000
British Pound	CME	7:20–2:00	BP 62,500	HMUZ	2 PTS = $12.50	1.00 = $625
British Pound	EFP	2:00PM–7:20AM	BP 62,500	HMUZ	2 PTS = $12.50	1.00 = $625
British Pound	MA	7:20–2:15 (9:31)	BP 12,500	HMUZ	2 PTS = $2.50	1.00 = $125
Canadian Dollar	CME	7:20–2:00 (9:16)	CD 100,000	HMUZ	1 PT = $10.00	1.00 = $1000
Canadian Dollar	EFP	2:00PM–7:20AM	CD 100,000	HMUZ	1 PT = $10.00	1.00 = $1000
Canadian Dollar	MA	7:20–2:15	CD 50,000	HMUZ	1 PT = $5.00	1.00 = $500
Deutsche Mark	CME	7:20–2:00 (9:16)	DM 125,000	HMUZ	1 PT = $12.50	1.00 = $1250
Deutsche Mark	EFP	2:00PM–7:20AM	DM 125,000	HMUZ	1 PT = $12.50	1.00 = $1250
Deutsche Mark	MA	7:20–2:15 (9:31)	DM 62,500	HMUZ	1 PT = $6.25	1.00 = $625
Japanese Yen	CME	7:20–2:00 (9:16)	JY 12,500,000	HMUZ	1 PT = $12.50	1.00 = $1250
Japanese Yen	EFP	2:00PM–7:20AM	JY 12,500,000	HMUZ	1 PT = $12.50	1.00 = $1250
Japanese Yen	MA	7:20–2:15 (9:31)	JY 6,250,000	HMUZ	1 PT = $6.25	1.00 = $625
Swiss Franc	CME	7:20–2:00 (9:16)	SF 125,000	HMUZ	1 PT = $12.50	1.00 = $1250
Swiss Franc	EFP	2:00PM–7:20AM	SF 125,000	HMUZ	1 PT = $12.50	1.00 = $1250
Swiss Franc	MA	7:20–2:15 (9:31)	SF 62,500	HMUZ	1 PT = $6.25	1.00 = $625
U.S. Dollar Index	NYCE	7:05–2:00 (9:00)	$1000 X INDEX	HMUZ	1 PT = $10.00	1.00 = $1000
ECU	NYCE	7:20–2:00 (9:00)	ECU 100,000	HMUZ	1 PT = $10.00	1.00 = $1000
Mexican Peso	CME	8:00–2:00	500,000	HMUZ	2.5 PTS = $12.50	1.00 = $500
Interest Rates						
Eurodollars	CME	7:20–2:00 (5:00AM)	$1,000,000	HMUZ	1/2 PT = $12.50	1.00 = $2500
Eurodollars	SMX	5:45PM–3:20AM CST 6:45PM–4:20AM CST	$1,000,000	HMUZ	1/2 PT = $12.50	1.00 = $2500
LIBOR CME	CME	7:20–2:00 (5:00AM)	$3,000,000	ALL	1 PT = $25.00	1.00 = $2500

(Continued)

TABLE 4.3 (Continued)

FINANCIAL FUTURES CONTRACT SPECIFICATIONS

Interest Rates (con't)

Municipal Bonds	CBOT	7:20–2:00	$1,000 X INDEX	HMUZ	1/32 = $31.25	1.00 = $1000
Treasury Bills	CME	7:20–2:00 (10:00)	$1,000,000	HMUZ	1 PT = $25.00	1.00 = $2500
Treasury Bills	MA	7:20–2:15 (10:15)	$500,000	HMUZ	1 PT = $12.50	1.00 = $1250
Treasury Bonds	CBOT	7:20–2:00 (12:00)	$100,000	HMUZ	1/32 = $31.25	1.00 = $1000
Treasury Bonds	MA	7:20–3:15 (12:00)	$50,000	HMUZ	1/32 = $15.625	1.00 = $500
Treasury Notes (10-Yr.)	CBOT	SAME AS T-BOND TIMES	$100,000	HMUZ	1/32 = $31.25	1.00 = $1000
Treasury Notes (10-Yr.)	MA	7:20–3:15 (12:00)	$50,000	HMUZ	1/32 = $15.625	1.00 = $500
Treasury Notes (5-Yr.)	CBOT	7:20–2:00 (12:00)	$100,000	HMUZ	1/64 = $15.625	1.00 = $1000
Treasury Notes (2-Yr.)	CBOT	7:20–2:00 (12:00)	$200,000	HMUZ	1/128 = $15.625	1.00 = $2000

Indices

CRB Index	NYFE	8:40–1:45 (2:15)	$500 X INDEX	FGJMQZX	5 PTS = $25.00	1.00 = $500
Eurotop 100	SMX	4:30AM–10:30AM (7:00)	$100 X INDEX	HMUZ	5 PTS = $10.00	1.00 = $100
Mid-Cap 400 Index	CME	8:30–3:15	$500 X INDEX	HMUZ	5 PTS = $25.00	1.00 = $500
Nikkei 225 Average	CME	8:00–3:15	$500 X INDEX	HMUZ	5 PTS = $25.00	1.00 = $500
NYFE Index	NYFE	8:30–3:15	$500 X INDEX	HMUZ	5 PTS = $25.00	1.00 = $500
S&P 500 Index	CME	8:30–3:15	$250 X INDEX	HMUZ	10 PTS = $25.00	1.00 = $250
KC Value Line Index	KCBT	8:30–3:15	$500 X INDEX	HMUZ	5 PTS = $25.00	1.00 = $500
Mini Value Line Index	KCBT	8:30–3:15	$100 X INDEX	HMUZ	5 PTS = $5.00	1.00 = $100
Goldman Sachs Index	CME	8:15–2:15	$250 X INDEX	ALL	10 PTS = $25.00	1.00 = $250
Russell 2000 Index	CME	8:30–3:15	$500 X INDEX	HMUZ	5 PTS = $25.00	1.00 = $500
Nasdaq 100 Index	CME	8:30–3:15	$100 X INDEX	HMUZ	5 PTS = $5.00	1.00 = $100
Dow Jones Ind. Avg.	CBOT	8:15–3:15	$10 X AVERAGE	HMUZ	1/2 PT = $5.00	1.00 = $10
E-Mini S&P 500	CME	24 HOURS EXCEPT:	$50 X INDEX	HMUZ	25 PTS = $12.50	1.00 = $.50

3:15PM–3:30PM MON- THUR; 3:15PM FRI–5:30PM SUN

Source: First American Discount Corporation, reprinted with permission.

Clearinghouse

A clearinghouse keeps track of all executed trades and marks customer accounts to market. The clearinghouse is an adjunct of an exchange. It also acts as an intermediary for every trade. Therefore, the buyers and sellers of the future do not come into contact with each other. Just as investors deposit margins at a broker, brokers and other clearinghouse members must deposit insurance money at a clearinghouse. This is called *clearing margins*. These margins are adjusted according to the profits/losses on the accounts that the brokers hold at the clearinghouse.

Rolling Futures Forward

Most financial futures expire every three months. If a trader has sold Treasury bonds that expire two years from now and intends to hedge them (hedging is covered later in this chapter) with buying Treasury bond futures, the trader will have to *roll the future forward* every three months. Rolling a future forward means selling the current one (e.g., the September future) and buying the later one (e.g., the December future). The price difference between the two is called *calendar spread*. There are traders who trade those types of spreads. Due to the fact that futures have a "fair value," some guidance is given as to whether the spread is expensive or cheap. (For details, refer to "The Fair Futures Price," later in this chapter.)

Types of Delivery

When an investor has an open futures position after the last trading day, a settlement has to take place. There are two ways of settling an open position after the last trading day: Physical settlement and Cash settlement.

Physical settlement means physically delivering the underlying asset or commodity. Most commodity futures are settled physically. For commodities, the arrangements for the delivery have to be specified. The New York Mercantile Exchange specifies the delivery of Heating oil as follows:

> "FOB (free on board) seller's facility, New York harbor ex-shore. All duties, entitlements, taxes, fees and other charges paid. Requirements for seller's shore facility: capability to deliver onto either trucks or barges at buyer's option. If delivery is taken by truck, the buyer pays a surcharge. Delivery must be made in intra-facility transfer. Delivery must be made in accordance with applicable federal, state, and local licensing and taxation laws."

For financial assets the delivery is easier. The underlying asset is deposited to the investment account of the buyer.

Most financial futures, such as the Dow future, are *cash settled*. That means that the difference between the futures price and the settlement price will be credited or debited to the investor's account. The reason for the cash settlement in the case of stock index futures is that physical delivery is sometimes impossible. Physically delivering the New York Composite Index future would mean delivering a portfolio of all stocks traded on the New York Stock Exchange.

The settlement price, also called exchange delivery settlement price (ESDP), is usually the last spot trading price. (A spot price is the price of an asset for immediate delivery.) Taking the last spot trading price (also called closing price) as the settlement price ensures that the future price equals the spot price at maturity of the future (see also Figure 4.4).

The S&P 500 is an exception to the rule that the delivery price is the last traded spot price. Here the settlement price is the opening price of the day after the last trading day. This is done to avoid manipulation of the settlement price on "triple witching day," a day when index futures, options on the index futures, and options on stocks expire.

In reality, most futures are *closed out* before the maturity date, so that no delivery of the underlying asset takes place. Closing out means entering into a futures trade that offsets the original trade. For example, a trader that has bought one Nikkei future contracts on January 13, at 20,500 will sell one Nikkei futures contract on February 13 at 21,000 to make a profit of $2,500. (One point in the Nikkei is $5 on the CME.) The trader will have no further obligation and no delivery will take place.

Types of Traders

Depending on the time horizon of realizing a profit, traders are divided into *scalpers, day traders* and *position traders.* Scalpers have a very short time horizon, trying to buy in and out of the market in minutes or seconds. Day traders close a position at the end of the day. Some banks advise their traders to do so, and not to hold overnight risks. Position traders trade long term and can hold open positions (a net long or short position of an asset) for more than a year.

Types of Orders

An investor's buy and sell orders can be given to a broker by telephone, Internet, or E-mail. Almost every brokerage company has Internet-based order facilities, E-mail registration, and E-mail order placement facilities. However, direct dealing, placing an order on the computerized futures trading system of an exchange, is not possible for a private investor. To trade a futures contract on an exchange, an exchange membership is necessary.

There are numerous types of orders given to a broker. The most common are as follows:

Market Order   When placing a market order an exact price is not specified by the investor. A market buy order termed, "Day order, buy one S&P 500 contract *at market*" assures that the floor broker will buy at the lowest offer available. Market sell orders assure a sell at the highest bid available. The term "day order" guarantees that the order will exist throughout the trading day. Market orders are the fastest way to trade, and fills (executed trades) are often received while the investor waits on the phone.

Limit Order   When placing a limit order an investor specifies the price and the size of the desired trade. A limit buy order termed, "Day order, buy one S&P 500 contract *at 710*" will guarantee a buy when the market trades lower than 710. When the market trades exactly at 710, the trade might not be executed, because with computerized trading, same price orders are filled on a first-come first-served basis.

Stop Order   When placing a stop order, this order becomes a market order if the market touches a certain price. Some years ago stop orders were only considered *stop loss orders*. Let's assume an investor has gone long (= has bought) the S&P 500 at a price of 1520. The investor believes that if the market drops below the support of 1500, it will fall further. Therefore the trader sets a stop a little lower than 1500, let's say 1495. If the market drops to 1495, the stop loss order will become a market order and the broker will sell at 1495 and stop the investor's losses.

Stop orders can also be *create profit orders*. Say an investor believes that if the resistance level of 1600 is broken, the market will rise further. So, the investor sets a buy order at 1605. Therefore, if the market trades at 1605, the investor will automatically buy the S&P at 1605.

A stop order price that is lower than the current market price is called MIT (market if touched). A stop order would be termed, "Day order, buy one S&P 500 *at 1610 stop.*"

Fill or Kill Order   With placing a fill or kill order, the broker will try to execute the order immediately. If he fails to execute it, the order will be canceled. The price of a fill or kill order should be close to the market price, in order to increase the likelihood of the execution. A fill and kill order is termed, "Day order, buy one S&P contract at 710 *fill or kill.*"

Order Cancels Order (OCO)   This order gives two prices to the broker. The trade will be executed at the price that the market touches first. After the trade has been executed, the whole order is canceled. An OCO makes sense, if an investor is long one contract of the S&P 500. He or she wants to sell at 1620, but thinks that when the market breaks 1600, it will go down further. So, the OCO is given, "Day order, sell one S&P 500 *at 1620, or at 1595 stop.*"

Commissions for Futures Trades

A broker is someone who invests your money until its gone.

—Woody Allen

Due to more efficient communications technology and increased competition, the commissions for trading futures are getting lower and lower. For a "round trip", that is, buying a contract and selling it later, or vice versa, discount brokers charge prices as low as $5 per contract with no further commissions. Other full service brokers that provide market analysis and investment advice charge up to $75 per round trip plus $150 commission per trade. Most brokerage companies have Internet trading facilities. The commission for Internet trading is usually lower than for telephone trading.

The Taxation of Futures

The most difficult thing in the world to understand is the income tax.

—Albert Einstein

In comparison to some European countries, where the use of futures as a speculation or hedge instrument is relevant, the taxation of futures in the United States is fairly straightforward. Open positions of futures at year-end are marked to market and treated as if they were realized profits and losses. Together with the actual profits and losses of future trades in that year, 60% of the gains are treated as long-term and 40% as short-term profits, irrespective of the actual holding period.

Profits and losses can be offset. Short-term profits and losses are offset against each other, and long-term profits and losses are offset against each other. Thus, a final short-term and a final long-term profit or loss figure will be derived.

Long-term profits are taxed at the personal income tax rate, with a maximum rate of 28%. Short-term profits are taxed at the personal income rate, with a maximum rate of 39.6%. Net losses are deductible against ordinary income up to $3,000. Losses over $3,000 can be carried forward to future years. Generally, commissions on future trades are deductible.

Main Features of the Dow Future

The future on the Dow Jones Industrial Average is a relatively new contract. It was established in October 1997. It trades on the CBOT (Chicago Board of Trade) and has the following key features.

Unit of Trading	$10 for each point of the Dow Jones Industrial Average
Minimum Price Fluctuation	One point ($10)
Trading Hours	8:15 a.m. to 3:15 p.m. (Central Standard time)·
Contract Months	March, June, September, and December
Last Trading Day	The day preceding the final settlement day
Final Settlement Day	The third Friday of the contract month
Position Limits	50,000 contracts net long or net short in all months combined
Daily Price Limits	Successive 10%, 20%, and 30% price limits. Price limits only apply to the downside.

| Settlement | Cash settlement on the final settlement day. The final settlement price is $10 times the special opening quotation of the index. |
| Ticker Symbol | DJ |

The contract months of March, June, September, and December indicate the month that the Dow future expires. The position limits, although large, exist to prevent excessive trading. If a trader really did have a 50,000 Dow future long position, it would mean that a one-point move in the Dow would lead to a $50,000 \times \$10 = \$500,000$ gain or loss. The daily price limits, which only apply to the downside, are implemented to prevent the market from falling sharply.

WHY ARE FUTURES SO POPULAR?

As illustrated in Figure 4.2, futures have become increasingly popular in recent years.

The decrease of futures trading in 1995 and 1996 on U.S. exchanges can be traced to three mitigating factors: maturing financial markets abroad, low volatility, and last but not least, bad press and derivatives scandals, as the Nick Leeson disaster ruining Barings Bank or the Orange County bankruptcy filing. Nevertheless, the overall trend of futures is up and should continue to be positive. There are three main reasons for the popularity of futures. First, futures are highly liquid, therefore the bid-offer spread is extremely narrow. Second, as seen above, futures are cheap. Third, futures have a leverage effect, which promises high returns at low costs. For these reasons, futures are a popular *speculation* tool, as well as an efficient *hedging* tool. An additional reason for the success of futures is *arbitrage*.

Let's examine those three tools briefly.

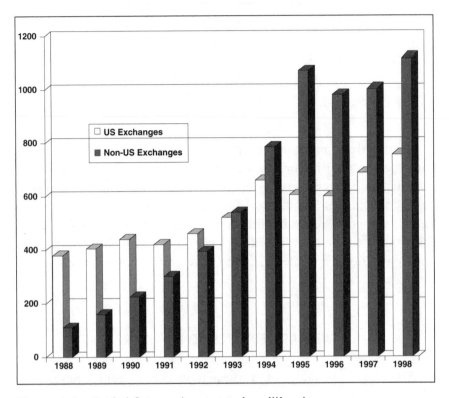

Figure 4.2   Traded futures (contracts in millions)
Source: Futures Industry (Magazine), February 1997.

Speculation

Speculation is buying or selling an asset to participate in the price movement of that asset. The difference in speculating with standard assets, such as stocks, versus speculating with futures on stocks is simple. When buying stocks, the investor has to come up with the money to buy them. When buying futures little initial cash is required, (just the margin money). Therefore, futures incorporate a *leverage effect,* promising high returns with very low capital input. The leverage effect of futures can be explained by looking at the cost-profit issue of a bond future. Formally, the leverage effect is:

$$\frac{\dfrac{\Delta P}{C_0}}{\dfrac{\Delta B}{B_0}} \quad \text{or} \quad \frac{\Delta P}{\Delta B} \frac{B_0}{C_0}$$

where

ΔP = change in the futures price

C_0 = cost of buying a futures contract

ΔB = change of the bond price

B_0 = initial bond price

EXAMPLE 4.3

Let's assume in a one-month period, the futures price at the beginning of the period is 98, the margin cost of buying a futures contract is 5% of the price, and the change of the futures price is +1. Also let the price of the bond at the beginning of the period be 100 and the change of the bond price +1. Following the previous equation, the leverage of the future for the past month is $1/(98 \times 0.05)/1/100 = 20.41$.

The example shows the leverage effect of futures, displaying the profit potential of a futures trade. A relative movement of the bond price of 1 leads to a relative profit of 20.41.

It is important to note however, that the leverage effect works against the investor if the underlying instrument moves in the undesired direction. There is no free lunch!

Hedging

Hedging is entering into a second trade to offset the risk of an original trade. Let's assume an investor has bought bonds from a trader, so that the trader has a short bond position. The trader, however, does not believe in decreasing bond prices and wants to hedge the price risk. The buyer could do so by buying treasury bond futures in order to neutralize the price risk. If the bond price increases, the trader will lose on the bond trade, but profit on the future; if the bond price decreases, the buyer takes a loss on the future, but will profit on the bond trade, thereby eliminating or reducing the price risk.

Arbitrage

Arbitrage is entering into two deals and deriving a profit without risk. The simplest form of arbitrage is buying and selling the same asset at the same point in time. For example, the JGB (Japanese Government Bond) future might trade on SIMEX (Singapore Monetary Exchange) 99.40–99.50. The same contract might trade on the Osaka exchange 99.55–99.65. This represents an arbitrage opportunity. A trader can buy the contract on SIMEX for 99.50 and sell it in Osaka for 99.55.

Another type of arbitrage involves time: If a future price is higher than its *fair value,* an investor can sell the future, buy the underlying asset, and hold the positions until the maturity date of the future.

THE FAIR FUTURES PRICE

The fair or arbitrage-free future price can be derived by *cost-of-carry* considerations. Cost-of-carry means analyzing the costs involved when holding the underlying asset and the future until future maturity.

The Fair Futures Price for an Asset without a Return

Gold pays no return in the form of a coupon or dividend. Let's assume the future of Gold expires in one month (31 days) and Gold trades at a spot price of $S = 320$. (The spot price is the price for immediate delivery, and so it is the price for any standard trade.) The spot Gold buyer who wants to sell Gold in one month will have to borrow cash for one month. If the one-month interest rate is $r = 5\%$, the Gold spot buyer has to pay:

$$S \times r \times n = 320 \times 0.05 \times 31/365 = 1.36$$

where

S = spot price of the underlying asset (= today's price)

r = refinancing interest rate

n = holding time of the future (in years)

Therefore, the fair futures price is:

$$F = S + 1.36 = 320 + 1.36 = 321.36.$$

This is the same as:

$$F = S (1 + r \times n) = 320 (1 + 0.05 \times 31/365) = 321.36$$

In conclusion, the spot price is lower than the futures price, because the spot gold buyer has to be compensated for having to borrow cash.

The Fair Futures Price for an Asset with a Return

If the underlying asset pays a return in the form of a dividend or coupon, the spot buyer benefits relative to the future buyer, because the spot buyer receives the return. Let's assume the price of the 30-year Treasury bond today is S = 99 and the coupon q = 8%. Because the coupon of a bond is paid on the par-value (the price at which the bond is issued and the price the bond will return to at maturity, in the absence of bankruptcy), for a one-month period the spot buyer will receive:

$$Sp \times q \times n = 100 \times 0.08 \times 31/365 = 0.68.$$

where

Sp = par value of the bond (usually 1000 in the United States and 100 in Europe and Asia)

Let's assume the one-month interest rate is 5%. Therefore, to finance the spot purchase of the bond the spot treasury buyer will have to pay:

$$S \times r \times n = 99 \times 0.05 \times 31/365 = 0.42.$$

Thus, the fair futures price F in one month is:

$$F = S + (S \times r \times n) - (Sp \times q \times n) = 99 + 0.42 - 0.68 = 98.74$$

Now the future price is lower than the spot price, because the future buyer is compensated for not receiving the coupon (which in our example over compensates the financing advantage of the future buyer).

Conversion of the Basis

The difference between the future price and the spot price of the underlying asset is called the *basis*. The basis is defined as the spot price of the underlying asset minus the futures price of that asset. Beware—in some publications, especially for financial assets, the reader will find the basis defined the opposite way (futures price minus spot price).

Figure 4.3 shows the conversion of the spot price S and the future price F, if the financing rate r is higher than the return of

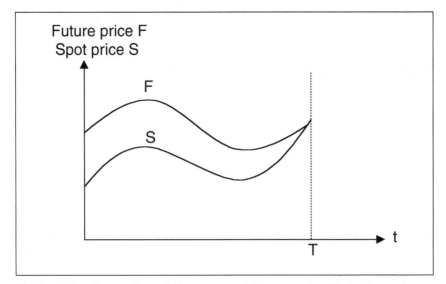

Figure 4.3 Conversion of the spot and futures price if the financing rate r is higher than the return q

the underlying asset q, or, if the underlying asset has no return, then q = 0. As shown in Figure 4.3, during the life of the future, the basis will narrow. This is because the time period and therefore the cost of financing the underlying asset purchase decreases. Mathematically, it is "n" that decreases (see previous fair futures price equations).

At the maturity of the future T, the spot price and the futures price are identical. This is because the future trade at T will be the same as the spot trade: If an investor sells a future on the last trading day T, he will have to deliver the underlying asset on the same day, as in a spot trade.

The future price F can also approach S from below (see Figure 4.4). This is the case when the coupon of the asset q is higher than the financing rate r. In other words, the Treasury bond buyer has an advantage over the Treasury future buyer, because the coupon on the bond is higher than the financing cost for the bond. For this advantage, the Treasury bond buyer will have to pay a premium in relation to the future, expressed as S – F.

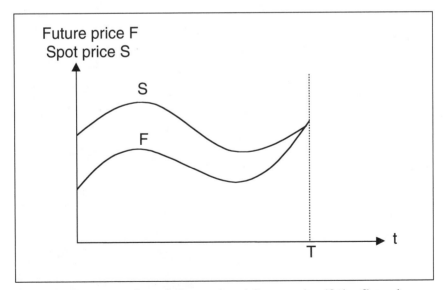

Figure 4.4   Conversion of the spot and future price if the financing rate r is lower than the return q

USING FUTURES

Following are six methods to outperform the Dow Jones Industrial Average using futures.

The Yield Curve Play

The yield of a bond is the return (= profit) gained if the bond is held to maturity. Therefore, the yield is a type of interest rate. The yield curve shows the yields of government bonds in relation to the maturity of those government bonds. Figure 4.5 shows the yield curve of the United States, Germany, and Japan. Japan, being in a recession in 1998, has very low yields to stimulate the economy. The U.S. curve is very flat. This means that buying long-term government bonds only pays a slightly higher profit than buying short-

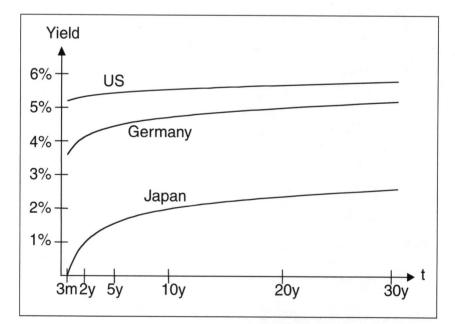

Figure 4.5 Yield curves of the United States, Germany, and Japan on July 15, 1998.

term bonds. A flat yield principally reflects a tight monetary policy and indicates the inflation concerns of the central bank, the Fed.

Method 4

The yield-curve play: Buy a Dow future and invest the cash saved in long-term bonds.

Why does buying a Dow future and investing the cash saved in long-term bonds outperform the Dow? In short, besides participating in the Dow gains via the Dow future, you will pay the low short-term interest rate of the yield curve and receive the higher long-term interest rate of the yield curve.

In this chapter, we have learned that the buyer of a future does not have to come up with much cash (just the margin). We have also learned that in the absence of returns, the fair market price of a future differs from the underlying asset price (the Dow) by the short-term interest or financing rate. We called this the cost-of-carry. In trading practice this financing rate or cost-of-carry is about the same as the short-term bond yield.

So, if we buy the expensive Dow future (F in Figure 4.3) instead of the Dow (S in Figure 4.3), we will lose the financing or carry-cost, which is represented by the financing rate or short-term bond yield r. However, since we bought a long-term bond, we are receiving the long-term coupon of that bond.

At the maturity of the future, the future on the Dow and the Dow will be identical (time T in Figure 4.3). Thus, we have participated in the Dow gains. Because the short-term interest rate is lower than the long-term rate (see Figure 4.5), our profit over the Dow is roughly the difference between the long-term and short-term interest rate. That's why the method is called the "yield curve play."

EXAMPLE OF METHOD 4

On March 20, the (spot) Dow is at 10,000 points. The Dow future will expire on June 18, (90 days). The short-term interest rate is 4%. The 30-year Treasury coupon is 6%. Using the fair futures price equation, it follows that the Dow future price is 10,000 × (1 + 0.04 × 90/365) = 10,099 points.

An investor has $100,000 and wants to beat the Dow. On March 20, he buys one Dow future at 10,099 and buys 6% Treasury bonds for $100,000.

One point in the Dow future represents $10. Thus, his carry loss is (10,099 – 10,000) × $10 × 1 contract = $990.

Let's assume the price of the Treasury bond is unchanged from March 20 to June 18. Thus on June 18, the investor can sell at the same price that he purchased the bond and make $100,000 × 0.06 × 90 / 365 = $1,479 on coupon income. Thus, the investor's overall profit is $1,479 – $990 = $489. In percentage terms this is $489 / $100,000 = 0.489%.

So, from March 20 to June 18, the investor has picked up an additional 0.489% over the Dow. This is roughly the same as the yield curve difference of (6%–4%) × $100,000 × 90 / 365 = $493. Without reinvesting this additional quarterly profit, the additional annual profit over the Dow is 0.489% × 4 = 1.956%.

It is important to mention that the investor will beat the Dow annually by 1.956%, wherever the Dow moves. If the Dow increases by 20%, the investor will make 20% + 1.956% = 21.956% profit with Method 4; if the Dow drops by 5%, the investor will lose 5% – 1.956% = 3.044% with Method 4.

The steeper the yield curve of an economy, the better Method 4 works. Thus in July 1998, Method 4 would work best in Japan, and not very well in the United States. However, the U.S. yield curve is usually steeper than the one in July 1998. (In July 1997 the three-month yield was 5.17% and the 30-year yield was 6.80%.)

Method 4 makes one crucial assumption. We have assumed that for the time of the investment, the Treasury bond price does not change. However, if the Treasury bond price decreases, Method 4 does not work as well. If the Treasury bond price drops below the yield-curve difference (in the previous example, more than 0.489%), Method 4 will underperform the Dow.

If, however, the Treasury bond price increases, Method 4 results in an even higher return over the Dow than the yield-curve difference.

Thus, the change of the Treasury bond price is the residual risk that the investor faces. We can replace this bond price risk with stock price risk. This leads to Method 5, which is often applied in trading practice.

Method 5

Buy the Dow future and invest the cash saved in stocks.

If we buy the Dow future and invest the cash saved in stocks, the outperformance of the Dow will be the stock price change minus the financing rate. In the United States, financing or short-term interest rates are currently low (the short-term bond yield is about 5.2%, as per Figure 4.5). This means that Method 5 works best if the stock price increase is higher than about 5.2% annually. This has been the case in the last five years.

EXAMPLE OF METHOD 5

On March 20 the (spot) Dow is at 10,000 points. The Dow future will expire on June 18, (90 days). The short-term interest rate is 4%. Again, using our futures equation, the Dow future price is 10,000 × (1 + 0.04 × 90/365) = 10,099 points.

An investor has $100,000 and wants to beat the Dow. On March 20, she buys one Dow future at 10,099 and buys Microsoft stock for $100,000. One point in the Dow future represents $10. Thus, her carry loss is (10,099 – 10,000) × $10 × 1 contract = $990.

Let's conservatively assume that Microsoft increases from March 20 to June 18 by 5%. (Microsoft has increased by 64% annually for the last five years.) So, the profit on Microsoft is $100,000 × 0.05 = $5,000. The overall profit over the Dow is $5,000 – $990 = $4,010. In percentage terms this is $4,010/$100,000 = 4.01%.

Without reinvesting this additional quarterly profit, the additional annual profit over the Dow is 4.01% × 4 = 16.04%.

It is again important to mention that (assuming Microsoft increases by 20% annually) the investor will beat the Dow annually by 16.04%, wherever the Dow moves. If the Dow increases by 30%, the investor will make 30% + 16.04% = 46.04% profit with Method 5; if the Dow drops by 5%, the investor will make 16.04% − 5% = 11.04% profit with Method 5.

The Tuesday Opportunity

The following analysis is based on closing prices for the last 30 years, from May 30, 1968 to May 30, 1998. The authors believe that any data earlier than this is too outdated to be relevant for predicting future investor behavior. Using data from the last 30 years, we have compiled a performance table of the Dow Jones Industrial Average (see Table 4.4).

From Table 4.4 we can see that Tuesday was by far the best trading day. Over the last 30 years the Dow increased on Tuesday by a total of 4,106.68 points or 51.19%. Thus the investor is advised to buy Dow future contracts at the close of Monday and sell them at the close of Tuesday or Wednesday. The Tuesday opportunity can be explained psychologically. On Monday traders and investors are often still in a weekend mood. They investigate their positions by looking at fundamental data and charts. Over the last 30 years, Monday has been the day with the lowest trading volume. On Tues-

TABLE 4.4 Absolute and Percentage Changes of the Dow from May 30, 1968 to May 30, 1998

	Observed Number of Days	Point Change of the Dow	Point Change of the Dow in Percent
Monday	1,450	+ 1,874.32	+ 23.34%
Tuesday	1,548	+ 4,106.68	+ 51.19%
Wednesday	1,527	+ 1,681.99	+ 20.94%
Thursday	1,515	− 738.19	− 9.19%
Friday	1,509	+ 1107.30	+ 13.79%
Sum	7,549	+ 8032.10	100%

day, the energy level rises and the outcome of the Monday-analysis leads to increased trading activity, which has resulted in a higher Dow in the past. There is no reason to believe that this established trading pattern will change in the near future.

It has also been empirically proven that most accidents in companies happen on Mondays and Fridays, because the employees are distracted by the previous or the upcoming weekend. In the nuclear industry, experiments are often done only Tuesday through Thursday, to minimize the risk of weekend distraction.

This theory might also help to explain the Thursday sell-off. As shown in Table 4.4, over the last 30 years the Dow has decreased on Thursdays by a total of 738.19 points or 9.19%. On Thursday, investors and traders tend to simply take some profits after the rise on Tuesday and Wednesday. (Friday is already a weekend-focused slow day with the second lowest daily trading volume after Monday.)

Table 4.4 leads us to Method 6:

Method 6

Buy a Dow future at the close of Monday and sell it at the close of Tuesday.

Using Method 6 the investor would have participated in 51.19% of the Dow gains in the last 30 years (as shown in Table 4.4). However, the daily performance of the Dow does vary for different time horizons. In the 1990s, Mondays and Tuesdays have been almost equally successful trading days. Table 4.5 shows the weekly/daily Dow performance in the 1990s.

Table 4.5 shows the Dow performance in the bull market of the 1990s. (Only 1990 was a down-year for the Dow, 1991 through 1998 were all up-years.) From Table 4.5 we derive Method 7.

Method 7

Buy a Dow future at the close of Friday and sell it at the close of Tuesday.

TABLE 4.5 Absolute and Percentage Changes of the Dow from March 29, 1990 to May 25, 1998

	Observed Number of Days	Point Change of the Dow	Point Change of the Dow in Percent
Monday	386	+3,157.22	51.51%
Tuesday	414	+3,165.48	51.65%
Wednesday	411	+391.29	6.38%
Thursday	405	−995.69	−16.25%
Friday	404	410.80	6.70%
Sum	2,020	+6,129.10	100.00%

With method 7 the investor would have participated in 23.34% + 51.19% = 74.53% of the Dow gains in the last 30 years (see Table 4.4). Also with Method 7, the investor would have participated in 51.51% + 51.65 = 103.16%! of the Dow gains in the last seven years (see Table 4.5).

Beware—the time period from 1990 to 1998 is somewhat short and may be distorted by the bull market.

Overall, the reader should look at the daily performance of the Dow with a certain degree of skepticism. In the future, investor behavior might change and result in different daily performances of the Dow.

Does "Tuesday Momentum" Exist? Since Tuesday is a pivotal day of the trading week (see Table 4.4), it seems sensible to investigate if a positive Tuesday is also a momentum day, meaning that a positive Tuesday has a follow-through effect on the next trading days. (Later in the book, we will derive the significant momentum effect of January). Table 4.6 shows the momentum for every trading day of the week.

From Table 4.6 we can see that Tuesday is not a momentum day and in fact, there is no significant momentum day. If anything,

TABLE 4.6 Six-day Momentum of Each Trading Day from May 30, 1968 to May 30, 1998

If Monday is up, next six days up (until Monday close)	If Tuesday is up, next six days up (until Tuesday close)	If Wednesday is up, next six days up (until Wednesday close)	If Thursday is up, next six days up (until Thursday close)	If Friday is up, next six days up (until Friday close)
53%	55%	59%	56%	59%

Wednesday and Friday seem to have a follow-through effect as the Dow increased in 59% of the cases.

The Triple Witching Opportunity

A triple witching day is a day on which three contracts expire:

- Option contracts on individual stocks
- Option contracts on indices (e.g., options on the Dow)
- Stock index future contracts (e.g., the Dow future)

A triple witching day occurs four times in a year, on the third Friday of March, June, September, and December.

A double witching day also exists. On a double witching day, the option contracts on individual stocks and option contracts on indices expire.

Testing the significance of double and triple witching days yields the results in Table 4.7.

Method 8

Buy a Dow future at the end of the trading day before a triple witching day, and sell it at the end of the triple witching day.

TABLE 4.7   Dow Changes of Double and Triple Witching Days from 1978 to 1998

	Absolute Change	Relative Change
Triple witching day	17.64	0.37%
Double witching day	14.13	0.36%
All other days	5.72	0.21%

As mentioned earlier, one point in the Dow future is equal to $10. By buying 10 Dow futures, the average profit of Method 8 in the last 20 years was $10 × 10 contracts × 17.64 = $1.764 per triple witching day.

Fool's Forecast—Basically for Fools Only

A very simple way to forecast stock prices is the fool's forecast. The method is derived from the weather forecast: If it is sunny today, it will be sunny tomorrow; if it is rainy today, it will be rainy tomorrow. According to meteorologists this is actually correct about 67% of the time. Because the stock market moves in trends, it is not unreasonable to assume a similar pattern for stocks. However, the fool's forecast works only a mediocre 54% for the stock market: If an investor buys a future on the close when the market had an up day, and sells it a day later on the close, the investor will only make money 54% of the time. In other words, in the last 30 years the market has had two consecutive up-days only 54% of the time.

For a down market the fool's forecast only works 51% of the time: If an investor sells a future at the close of the market after a down day, and buys it back a day later at the close, the investor will only make money 51% of the time. In other words, in the last 30 years the market has had two consecutive down-days only 51% of the time.

However, the fool's forecast can be somewhat improved. If we only take days where the market has moved up more than 1%, the fool's forecast works 58% of the time. This brings us to Method 9.

Method 9

Buy a Dow future at the end of the trading day if the Dow has moved up by more than 1%, and sell it at the end of the next trading day.

As mentioned, Method 9 has worked 58% of the trading days over the last 30 years. In terms of Dow points, of the 58% up-up days, the Dow has moved, on average, 15 points up the second day. Of the 42% up-down days, the Dow has lost, on average, 11 points on the second day.

Not surprisingly, Method 9 has worked slightly better in the bull market of the 1990s. From 1990 to 1998, in 60% of all cases, the Dow had two consecutive up days if the first day was up more than 1%.

Following the logic of Method 9, we derive Method 10.

Method 10

Sell a Dow future at the end of the trading day if the Dow has dropped more than 1%, and buy it back at the close of the next trading day.

Method 10 has worked 57% of the time over the last 30 years. In terms of Dow points, of the 57% down-down days, the Dow has moved down, on average, 16 points the second day. Of the 43% down-up days, the Dow has gained, on average, 17 points on the second day.

As to be expected, Method 10 does not work as well in the bull market of the 1990s. From 1990 to 1997, the Dow has decreased 51% of the time after a down day of more than 1%.

SUMMARY

This chapter explained how futures work and showed several ways to outperform the Dow Jones Industrial Average using futures.

A future is the agreement to trade the underlying asset at a certain date in the future, at a price that is determined today. A future can be viewed as a bet. The future buyer is betting that the underlying asset price will be higher than the traded future price, the future seller is betting that the underlying asset price will be lower than the traded future price at future maturity.

All futures trades are executed at the current future price. The current future price is derived by supply and demand in the market. Thus, it is considered a fair mid-market price to trade the underlying asset at the maturity date of the future. Therefore, the future buyer does not pay a premium to the future seller at the time the future is traded. Rather, the future buyer will pay the future price to the future seller at future maturity and receive the underlying asset from the future seller.

Regarding futures, the distinction between price and value is important. At the time of the trade, the Dow future might have a price of 11,000 Dow points. However, at the exact moment the future is traded, the value of the future trade is zero. The value of a future trade changes if the future price changes. If a Dow future was bought at a price of 11,000 and the Dow future price moves to 11,500, the value of the future trade is $(11,500 - 11,000) \times \$10 = \$5,000$.

The clearinghouse is an adjunct of an exchange. The clearinghouse marks-to-market every future trade of every investor. This means that the profit or loss of every future trade is calculated at the end of the trading day. If an investor loses money on a future transaction and his account drops below a predefined maintenance margin, the investor has to deposit more money into his account to meet the initial margin. If an investor fails to meet the initial margin, the clearinghouse has the right to cancel the investor's future position.

There are two types of settlement of the future transaction at the maturity date of the future. Physical settlement means that the future buyer will pay the future price and will physically receive the underlying asset. For example, in a live cattle future trade, the future seller has to deliver the live cattle to the future buyer. Most commodity futures are physically settled.

All financial futures, such as the Dow future, have a cash settlement. This means that the difference between the future trading price and the future price at future maturity is credited or debited to the investor's account. For example, if an investor had sold one Dow future at 11,000 Dow points and the Dow future is 11,200 at future maturity, the debited loss for the investor will be (11,200 − 11,000) × $10 = $2,000.

There are several types of orders when trading a future.

In a market order the investor specifies no price. The future will be bought at the lowest available offer or sold at the highest available bid. Market orders are the fastest and surest way to trade, and fills (executed trades) are often received within seconds. In a limit order the investor specifies the price at which the future should be bought or sold. This trade is not guaranteed. The order is usually alive until the end of the trading day. A stop order becomes alive if the market touches a certain price. Stop orders are often used to hedge; If an investor has bought a Dow future at 11,000, and has placed a stop at 10,000, his future will be sold at 10,000 if the Dow future has traded at 10,000. In an order cancels order (OCO), two prices are given to the broker. The trade is executed at the price that the Dow future trades at first.

Futures are used for speculation because of their leverage. Leverage is the profit potential relative to the capital input. Since trading futures is free (except for the margin money), futures incorporate a high leverage. Futures are also a popular hedging (risk-reduction) tool, because they are liquid, easy to trade, and cheap. The fair future price can be easily calculated from cost-of-carry considerations. Due to the fact that the future price and the spot price are equal at future maturity, futures are also used for arbitrage if the fair future price differs from the actual future price.

Due to the historical patterns that the Dow has taken over the last 30 years, there are several methods to outperform the Dow using futures. The popular yield curve play allows an investor to receive a high long-term yield and to pay a low short-term yield. The modified method of the yield curve play is paying a short-term yield and receiving the return of a certain stock.

In the last 30 years, 51.19% of the 7,529 Dow point gain has occurred on a Tuesday. Therefore, the Tuesday opportunity is buying a Dow future on Monday's close and selling it on Tuesday's close. This method would have achieved a $75,290 profit.

Triple witching days, are days on which option contracts on individual stocks, option contracts on indixes (e.g., options on the Dow), and stock index future contracts (e.g., the Dow future) expire. These days represent a unique trading opportunity. While the average daily increase of the Dow was 5.72 points, on triple witching days the Dow increased, on average, by 17.64. Thus, buying a future before a triple witching day and selling it at the close of the triple witching day is opportune.

The fool's forecast tries to exploit trends in the Dow (i.e., buying one day after a Dow increase) but it has a mediocre 54% success rate. The modified fools forecast (i.e., buying one day after the Dow has increased more than 1%) exploits the popular follow-through effect with a 58% success rate.

Using the suggested methods naturally assumes a repetitive investor behavior. There is ample evidence that investors repeat successful trading strategies and engage in repetitive cyclical behavior. Therefore, the suggested methods should work in the long run. Naturally, there is no guarantee that the suggested methods will work for certain specific time periods.

SUGGESTED READING

Andersen, T., (1993). *Currency and Interest Rate Hedging; A User's Guide to Options, Futures, Swaps & Forward Contracts,* (New York: New York Institute of Finance).

Brown, B., (1983). *The Forward Market in Foreign Exchange: A Study in Market-Making, Arbitrage, and Speculation,* (New York: St. Martin's Press).

Chicago Board of Trade, (1987). "Interest Rate Futures for Institutional Investors," (Chicago).

Figlewski, S., (1986). *Hedging with Financial Futures for Institutional Investors: From Theory to Practice,* (Cambridge, MA: Ballinger Pub. Co.).

Hillsdon, B., (1977). "Hedging against inflation: Anticipating the future: A Business Guide to Managing the Effects of Cost, Price and Parity

Changes," (Melbourne: Committee for Economic Development of Australia).

Jaffe, N., (1979). "Survey of Interest-rate Futures Markets," (Washington, D.C.: Commodity Futures Trading Commission, Division of Economics and Education).

Jones, E., (1987). *Hedging Foreign Exchange: Converting Risk to Profit,* (New York: John Wiley & Sons).

Koziol, J., (1990). *Hedging: Principles, Practices, and Strategies for the Financial Markets,* (New York: John Wiley & Sons).

Loosigian, A., (1980). *Interest Rate Futures,* (Homewood, IL: Dow Jones-Irwin).

Meissner, G., (1998). *Trading Financial Derivatives, Futures, Swaps and Options in Theory and Application,* (New York: Simon and Schuster).

Pitts, M., (1990). *Interest Rate Futures and Options,* (Chicago, IL: Probus Pub. Co.).

Siegel, D., (1990). *The Futures Markets: Arbitrage, Risk Management and Portfolio Strategies,* (Chicago, IL: Probus Pub. Co.).

Venkataramanan, L., (1965). *The Theory of Futures Trading: Hedging, Speculation, and Storage in Organized Commodity Markets,* (New York: Asia Pub. House).

5

OUTPERFORMING THE DOW USING STANDARD OPTIONS

If everything goes wrong, trade options.

OPTIONS: AN INTRODUCTION

What is an *option?* In broad terms, an option is the right do to something.

Options can be divided into calls and puts. A *call* is the right, but not the obligation, to buy a certain asset at a predetermined price (strike), on a predetermined date (European style) or during a predetermined time period (American style). A *put* is the right, but not the obligation, to sell a certain asset at a predetermined price (strike), on a predetermined date (European style) or during a predetermined time period (American style).

For the right to buy or sell the underlying asset, the option buyer pays a price, the *option premium,* to the option seller. As in a common purchase, the price is usually paid at the time of the purchase.

Exercising an option is utilizing the right that the option buyer has. An option is exercised if it is beneficial for the option buyer. For example, if the call buyer has the right to buy Microsoft at $100 (strike), and Microsoft has a market value of higher than $100, then the call buyer will exercise the call and buy Microsoft at $100 from the option seller. If the put buyer has the right to sell Microsoft at $100, and Microsoft trades lower than $100, the put buyer will exercise the put and sell Microsoft at $100 to the option seller.

Therefore, only the option *buyer* has a *right*. He has the right to buy or sell the underlying asset. The option *seller* has the *obligation* to complete the trade, if the option buyer decides to exercise his right.

The difference between a future and an option lies in the fact that the option buyer has the *right* to buy or sell the underlying asset, whereas the future buyer *and* seller have the *obligation* to buy or sell the asset in the future. Thus an option will lead to a *potential* purchase or sale of the underlying asset. A future will *certainly* lead to a trade in the future.

Options have a *maturity date*. For a European style option, the maturity date is the *only* date at which the option can be exercised. For an American style option the maturity date is the *last* date the option can be exercised. So, American style options can be exercised any time from the purchase date to the maturity date. Naturally, American style options are more expensive or as expensive as European style options. On the American exchanges, European style and American style options are traded.

TRADING OPTIONS

In all four major markets, the commodity, currency, equity, and fixed income market, there is a highly liquid option market. A private investor who wants to buy a call or a put on a commodity or a standard asset, like Gold, the Yen, the IBM stock, or a stock index, will not have any problems getting bid-offer spreads from any major U.S. or international investment bank.

Exchange traded options are also extremely popular. Tables 5.1 and 5.2 show the most popular options traded in the United States.

Options on commodity futures (Table 5.1) are divided into options on Metals, Energies, Grains and Legumes, Meats, and Exotics. Options on financial futures (Table 5.2) are categorized in currencies, interest rates, and types of indices.

Quotes on these options can be viewed free of charge on www.CBOE.com, go to Delayed Quotes, or www.cme.com, go to Free Live Quotes.

Options expire usually monthly as seen in column 5 in Tables 5.1 and 5.2 (ALL). The expiration day is the third Friday of the relevant month. For the explanations on the major exchanges (column 2) and the expiration months (column 5), refer back to Chapter 4.

In many respects, trading options on an exchange is similar to trading futures. A clearinghouse manages and settles all executed trades and calculates the margin requirements. The option contracts are standardized in terms of contract size, strike levels, expiration date, etc. Position limits exist to prevent excessive trading.

Buying and Selling Options

An option buyer does not have to wait until his option matures. An option can be bought and sold any time before option maturity. An active market with narrow bid-offer margins exists on the major exchanges. The types of orders to buy and sell options are the same as the orders for futures (refer back to Chapter 4.)

Exercising an Option

Exercising an option means that the option buyer informs the option seller (usually by phone) that the right implied by the option contract is executed. A European style option can only be exercised on the day of option maturity. An American style option can be exercised any time before option maturity. If an investor informs the clearinghouse that he wants to exercise his option, the clearinghouse randomly chooses the option seller out of all possible option sellers.

TABLE 5.1 Options on Commodity Futures Specification

OPTIONS ON COMMONDITY FUTURES

Metals	Exch	Hours(Ltd.)	Size	Months	Fluctuation	Strike prices
Copper	CMX	7:10–1:00	25,000 LBS	HKNUZ	.05 CT/LB = $12.50	Every 2CT/LB
Gold	CMX	7:20–1:30	100 OZ	ALL	.10/OZ = $10.00	Every $10/OZ
Platinum	NYME	7:20–1:30	50 OZ	ALL	.10/OZ = $5.00	Every $10/OZ
Silver, NY	CMX	7:25–1:25	5,000 OZ	ALL	.10 CT/OZ = $5.00	Every 25 CT/OZ
Silver, New	CBOT	7:25–1:25	1,000 OZ	GJMQVZ	.10 CT/OZ = $1.00	Every 25 CT/OZ
Energies						
Crude Oil	NYMEX	8:45–2:10 (1:40–2:10)	$.01BBL	ALL	1 PT = $10.00	Every $.50/BBL
Heating Oil	NYMEX	8:50–2:10 (1:40–2:10)	.01¢/GAL	ALL	1 PT = $4.20	Every 1CT/GAL
Unleaded Gas	NYMEX	8:50–2:10 (1:40–2:10)	.01¢/GAL	ALL	1 PT = $4.20	Every 1CT/GAL
Natural Gas	NYMEX	9:00–2:10 (2:10)	.1c/MMBTU	ALL	1 PT = $10.00	Every 5CT/MMBTU
Electricity	NYMEX	8:55–2:30	736 MWH/MONTH	ALL	$.01/MWH = $7.36	
Grains & Legumes						
Corn	CBOT	9:30–1:15 (12:00)	5,000 BU	HKNUZ	$1/8$ CT/BU = $6.25	Every 10 CT/BU
Oats	CBOT	9:30–1:15	5,000 BU	HKNUZ	$1/8$ CT/BU = $6.25	Every 10 CT/BU
Soybeans	CBOT	9:30–1:15 (12:00)	5,000 BU	FHKNUQX	$1/8$ CT/BU = $6.25	Every 25 CT/BU
Soybeans	MA	9:30–1:45 (12:15)	1,000 BU	FHKNUQX	$1/8$ CT/BU = $1.25	Every 25 CT/BU
Soybeans Meal	CBOT	9:30–1:15 (12:00)	100 TONS	FHKNQUV	5 CT/TON = $5.00	Every $10/TON
Soybeans Oil	CBOT	9:30–1:15 (12:00)	60,000 LBS	FHKNQUV	.00005 CT/LB = $3.	Every 1 CT/LB
Wheat	CBOT	9:30–1:15 (12:00)	5,000 BU	HKNUZ	$1/8$ CT/BU = $6.25	Every 10 CT/BU
Wheat	KCBT	9:30–1:15	5,000 BU	HKNUZ	$1/8$ CT/BU = $6.25	
Wheat	MGE	9:30–1:15	5,000 BU	HKNUZ	$1/8$ CT/BU = $6.25	
Wheat	MA	9:30–1:45 (12:15)	1,000 BU	HKNUZ	$1/8$ CT/BU = $6.25	

Meats						
Cattle, Feeders	CME	9:05–1:00 (12:00)	50,000 LBS	FHJKQUV	2 $\frac{1}{2}$ PT = $12.50	Every 1CT/LB
Cattle, Live	CME	9:05–1:00 (12:00)	40,000 LBS	GJMQVZ	2 $\frac{1}{2}$ PT = $10.00	Every 1CT/LB
Hogs, Lean	CME	9:10–1:00 (12:00)	40,000 LBS	GJMQVZ	2 $\frac{1}{2}$ PT = $10.00	Every 1CT/LB
Pork Bellies	CME	9:10–1:00 (12:00)	40,000 LBS	GHKNQX	2 $\frac{1}{2}$ PT = $10.00	Every 1CT/LB
Exotics						
Cocoa	CSCE	8:00–1:00	10 METRIC TONS	HKNUZ	1 PT = $10.00	Every $50/TON
Coffee	CSCE	8:15–12:32	37,500 LNBS	HKNUZ	1 PT = $3.75	Every 5CT/LB
Cotton	NYCE	9:30–1:40 (11:30)	50,000 LBS	HKNVZ	.01C/LB = $5.00	Every 1CT/LB F 3MOS
Lumber	CME	9:00–1:05 (12:05)	80,000 BD/FT	FHKNUX	1 PT = $8.00	Every 5CT/BD/FT
Orange Juice	NYCE	9:15–1:15 (11:00)	15,000 LBS	FHKNUX	.05C/LB = $7.50	Every 5C/LB
Sugar	CSCE	8:30–12:20	112,000 LBS	HKNVZ	1 PT = $11.20	Every $\frac{1}{2}$CT/LB
Rice	CBOT	9:15–1:30	2,000 CWT	FHKNUX	1/4C/CWT = $5.00	Every 20CT/LB

Source: First American Discount Corporation.

TABLE 5.2 Financial Options Contact Specifications

OPTIONS ON FINANCIAL FUTURES

	Exch.	Hours (Ltd.)	Size	Months	Fluctuation	Strikes
Currencies						
Australian Dollar	CME	7:20–2:00 (9:16)	100,000 AD	ALL	1 PT = $10.00	Every 1 CT
British Pound	CME	7:20–2:00	62,500 BP	ALL	2 PT = $12.50	Every 1 CT
Canadian Dollar	CME	7:20–2:00 (9:16)	100,000 CD	ALL	1 PT = $10.00	Every 1/2 CT
Deutsche Mark	CME	7:20–2:00 (9:16)	125,000 DM	ALL	1 PT = $12.50	Every 1/2 CT
Japanese Yen	CME	7:20–2:00 (9:16)	12,500,000 JY	ALL	1 PT = $12.50	Every 1/2 CT
Swiss Franc	CME	7:20–2:00 (9:16)	125,000 SF	ALL	1 PT = $12.50	Every 1/2 CT
U.S. Dollar Index	NYCE	7:05–2:00 (9:00)	1000 × US$ IND.	ALL	1 PT = $10.00	Every 1 CT
Interest Rates						
Eurodollar	CME	7:20–2:00 (5AM OR 2PM)	$1,000,000 ED	ALL	1/2 PT = $12.50	Every 25 PTS
LIBOR	CME	7:20–2:00 (5AM OR 2PM)	$3,000,000	ALL	1/2 PT = $12.50	Every 25 PTS
Municipal Bond	CBOT	7:20–2:00	$1000 × INDEX	HMUZ	1/64 PT = $15.625	Every 1 BASIS PT
Treasury Bill	CME	7:20–2:00 (10:00)	$1,000,000	ALL	1 PT = $25.00	Every 25 PTS
Treasury Bond	CBOT	7:20–2:00 (12:00) 5:20PM–8:05PM CST 6:20PM–9:05PM CDT 10:00PM–6:00AM PROJECT A	$100,000	ALL	1/64 PT = $15.625	Every 1 BASIS PT
Treasury Note	CBOT	7:20–2:00 (12:00) 5:20PM–8:05PM CST 6:20PM–9:05PM CDT	$100,000	ALL	1/64 PT = $15.625	Every 1 BASIS PT
Indices						
CRB	NYFE	8:40–2:15	$500 × CRB IND.	FGJMQ	5 PTS = 25.00	Every 200 PTS
Eurotop 100	CMX	4:30–10:30AM (7:00)	$100 × INDEX	HMUZ	1 PT = $10.00	Every 1000 PTS
Nikkei	CME	8:00–3:15	$5 × NIKKEI AVE.	ALL	5 PTS = 25.00	Every 500 PTS
NY Com. Index	NYFE	8:30–3:15	$500 × NYSE IND.	ALL	5 PTS = 25.00	Every 200 PTS
S&P 500 Index	CME	8:30–3:15	$250 × S&P IND.	ALL	10 PTS = $25.00	Every 500 PTS
Nasdaq 100 Ind.	CME	8:30–3:15	$100 × INDEX	ALL	5 PTS = $5.00	Every 100 PTS
DJIA	CBOT	8:15–3:15	$10 × INDEX	ALL	1/2 PT = $5.00	Every 100 PTS
E-Mini S&P 500	CME	24 HOURS EXPECT: 3:15PM–3:30PM M-TH; 3:15PM F-5:30PM S	$50 × INDEX	ALL	.25 PT = $12.50	5-point intervals for nearest 2 contr 10-point intervals for deferred months

Source: First American Discount Corporation.

It is important to mention that it is usually better to *sell* an option than to *exercise* it early. This is because the time value (= profit potential) is lost when exercising an option prematurely.

Options on exchanges owned by individuals are exercised automatically, if they are "in the money" (if they have a positive payoff; see Figures 5.1 through 5.4) by a certain amount. This amount varies from exchange to exchange.

Margins

Since the maximum loss the option buyer faces is the option premium, the initial risk margin of an option purchase is the option premium.

For an option seller, the margin on most exchanges is the current premium plus 15% of the index value. If the option is going "out of the money" (loses value), the margin is reduced to the current option value, plus 10% of the current index value.

Settlement

Options can be physically settled or cash settled. Physical settlement means that the call buyer will pay the strike price and buy the underlying asset; the put buyer will receive the strike price and has to deliver the underlying asset.

Stock index options are cash settled. That means that the difference between the strike and the price of the underlying asset is paid in cash from the option seller to the option buyer. Let's assume that the Dow trades at 11,500. Thus, an investor who has bought a call on the Dow with a strike of 11,000 receives (11,500 − 11,000) = $500 in cash from the option seller when he or she exercises the call.

Stock Index Options

The most popular index future option contracts listed on U.S. exchanges are options on the Dow Jones Industrial Average (DJIA) (in this book, the "Dow"), the S&P 100, the S&P 500, the Nasdaq 100, the Amex Market Value Index (AMVI), and the New York Stock Exchange Index (NYSE).

Options on the Dow Jones Industrial Average

Let's look briefly at the specification of options on the Dow, which trade on the CBOE (Chicago Board of Option Exchange).

Style	European style
Underlying Instrument	1/100 of DJIA (= Dow). (So if the DJIA trades at 10,500, the underlying is 105.)
Minimum Price Fluctuation	Series trading below $3 is $1/16^{th}$, above $3 is $1/8^{th}$
Multiplier	$100 (So if quoted price is 2 1/2, the option premium is $2.5 \times \$100 = \$250$)
Trading Hours	8:30 a.m. to 3:15 p.m. (Central Standard time)
Contract Months	Monthly (The maturity date is the third working Friday of every month.)
Last Trading Day	The business day (usually a Thursday) preceding the final settlement day
Final Settlement Day	The third Friday of the contract month
Settlement	Cash settlement on the final settlement day. (If the settlement price is 107 and the call strike is 105, the call buyer receives $107 - 105 \times \$100 = \$200$.)
Ticker Symbol	DJX

Warrants

Warrants are securitized options for the small investor. The term "securitized" simply means that the private investor receives a certificate for the trade. Often $100 is enough to buy a call or a put warrant. Because of the high risk when selling options, investors are usually not allowed to have a short (selling) position in warrants. Naturally, an investor can sell a warrant in order to close a long (buying) position.

Call and put warrants are often issued by a company on their own stock or bonds. After their first issue, they are often listed and managed on an exchange. The lifetime of warrants is usually longer than that of standard options. One-to three-year warrants are often issued.

Options at Maturity: The Hockey Sticks

A good understanding of options is gained when we look at the payoff of an option at option maturity. Four types of diagrams result: Bought (long) call, sold (short) call, bought (long) put, and sold (short) put.

In Figure 5.1 an investor is *long a call* (has bought a call). In Figure 5.1, the investor has paid $10 for a call with a strike of $100. Thus, the investor has the right to buy the underlying stock at $100. The investor will exercise that right and buy the stock at $100 if the call is "in the money," i.e., if the stock has a price of more than $100. The investor will usually not exercise the call and not buy the stock at $100 if the call is "at the money," i.e., if the underlying stock price is at $100. The investor will not exercise the call and not buy the stock at $100 if the underlying stock price is below $100. In this case the investor loses his investment of $10.

As shown in Figure 5.1, the maximum loss that the call buyer faces is the option premium of $10. The maximum profit is unlimited. The break-even point is at $110—the strike price of $100 plus the premium of $10.

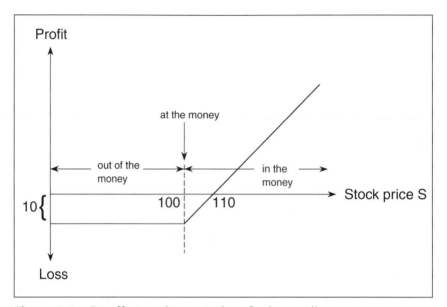

Figure 5.1   Payoff at option maturity of a long call

The payoff in Figure 5.2 is that of a *sold (short) call*. This payoff is obtained by reflecting the call buyer's payoff at the zero line:

As shown in Figure 5.2, the call seller's maximum profit is the option premium of $10. This profit of $10 is achieved if the call finishes "out of the money," i.e., if the stock price is below $100 and the call buyer does not exercise the call. The profit of $10 is also achieved if the call finishes "at the money," i.e., if the stock price is at $100. In this case the call buyer will usually not exercise the call. If the option finishes "in the money" the loss for the call seller depends on the price of the underlying stock. The higher the stock price, the more the call seller loses. The maximum loss for the call seller is unlimited!

The break-even stock price for the call seller (and the call buyer) is $110, the strike price of $100 plus the premium of $10.

In Figure 5.3, an investor is *long a put* (has bought a put). The investor has paid $10 for a put with a strike of $100. Thus, the investor has the right to sell the underlying stock at $100.

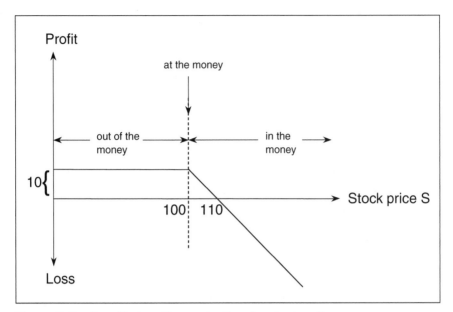

Figure 5.2 Payoff at option maturity of a short call

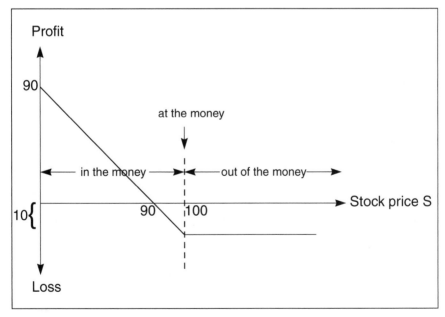

Figure 5.3 Payoff at option maturity of a long put

The investor will exercise that right and sell the stock at $100 if the put is "in the money," i.e., if the stock has a price of less than $100. The investor usually will not exercise the put and not sell the stock at $100 if the put is "at the money," i.e., if the underlying stock price is at $100. The investor will not exercise the put and not sell the stock at $100 if the put is "out of the money," i.e., if the underlying, stock price is above $100. In this case the investor loses his investment of $10.

The maximum loss that the put buyer faces is the option premium $10. The maximum profit is achieved when the stock price goes to zero. In that case the investor sells the stock at $100. By deducting the option premium of $10, the maximum profit is $90. The break-even stock price is the strike price of $100 minus the option premium of $10, which is also $90.

The payoff in Figure 5.4 is that of a *sold (short) put*. This payoff is obtained reflecting the put buyer's payoff at the zero line:

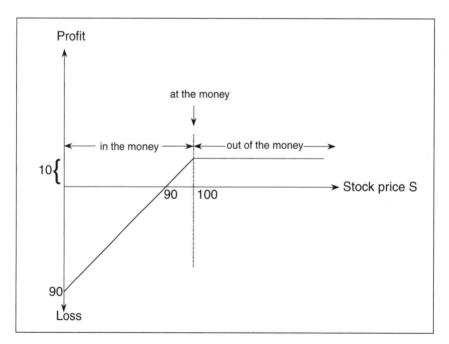

Figure 5.4 Payoff at option maturity of a short put

As shown in Figure 5.4, the maximum profit of the put seller is the option premium of $10.

This profit of $10 is achieved if the put finishes "out of the money," i.e., if the stock price is above $100 and the put buyer does not exercise the put. The profit of $10 is also achieved if the put finishes "at the money." In this case the stock price is at $100 and the put buyer will usually not exercise the put. If the put finishes "in the money," i.e., if the stock price is below $100, the loss for the put seller depends on the price of the underlying stock. Since the stock price can only go to zero, the maximum loss for the put seller is $100 minus the received option price of $10, or $90.

The break-even point for the put seller (and the put buyer) is the strike price of $100 minus the premium of $10, therefore $90.

From the payoffs in Figure 5.1 through 5.4 we conclude that selling options is a dangerous thing to do! The maximum loss is unlimited in the case of a call, and high in the case of a put (strike minus premium).

It is therefore not surprising that in the past, exchanges have not allowed a private investor to sell options. Recently, however, exchanges have liberalized selling options. On the Chicago Board of Option Exchange, a private investor can sell options if he deposits a margin of the option premium plus 15% of the premium.

Option Strategies

The four basic option payoffs can be combined to create option strategies. One of the most famous strategies is the straddle.

The Long Straddle   Figure 5.5 shows a long (bought) straddle: a long call and a long put with the same strike and same option maturity. The reader may wonder why it makes sense to buy a call *and* a put. The answer is given in Figure 5.5. In this figure, "a" is the long call, and "b" is the long put as in Figures 5.1 and 5.3. The resulting graph "c" is the payoff of a long straddle.

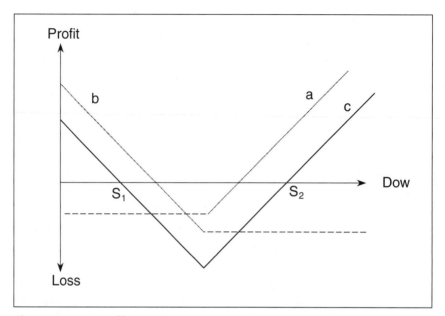

Figure 5.5 Payoff at option maturity of a long straddle

From Figure 5.5 we can see that the long straddle generates a profit if the stock price S is lower than S_1 or higher than S_2. Therefore, buying a straddle is sensible if an investor expects high volatility of the underlying stock, but is not sure if the price will increase or decrease sharply. In Figure 5.5 the put is slightly more expensive than the call. This is often the case because stocks tend to drop more sharply than they rise.

The Short Straddle   Figure 5.6 shows a short (sold) straddle. A short straddle is a short call and a short put with the same strike and maturity. The payoff is given in Figure 5.6: "a" is the short call, and "b" is the short put as in Figures 5.2 and 5.4. The resulting graph "c" is the payoff of a short straddle.

From Figure 5.6 we can see that the short straddle generates a profit if the stock price S is higher than S_1 and lower than S_2. Therefore, selling a straddle is sensible if an investor expects low volatility of the underlying stock.

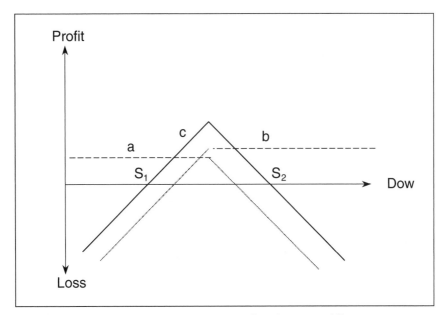

Figure 5.6 Payoff at option maturity of a short straddle

In Figure 5.6, as in Figure 5.5, the put is slightly more expensive than the call. Again, this is often the case because stocks tend to drop more sharply than they rise.

Covered Call Writing

Another popular option strategy is *covered call writing*. If an investor is long an asset, but believes the upside potential of the asset is limited over the short term, the investor can sell a call to increase the investment return. In Figure 5.7, "a" represents being long the stock and "b" is the short call. Adding "a" and "b" yields "c", the payoff of a covered call writing.

Comparing the covered call writing "c" with being long the asset "a", it is easy to see that the covered call writing strategy is superior to just holding the stock, if the price of the asset is lower than 110. If the price is above 110, just holding the stock is more profitable than a covered call writing strategy. Thus, a covered call writing strategy

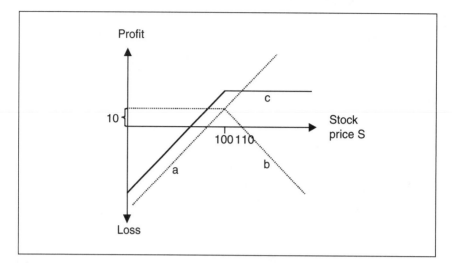

Figure 5.7   Payoff at maturity of the covered call writing strategy

is sensible if the investor believes the asset is a good position in the long run, but wants to increase his short-term return. (The attentive reader will have noticed that a covered call writing strategy is identical to selling a put, as shown in Figure 5.4.)

WHY ARE OPTIONS SO POPULAR?

Speculation, hedging, and arbitrage are the main reasons for the success of options. In the following sections, we'll look at these three aspects.

Options as Speculation Instrument—The Leverage Effect

Options are a popular speculation instrument because they are cheap and promise high returns. The relationship between costs and returns is measured by the leverage effect. Table 5.3 examines the leverage effect of an option in a numerical example.

Table 5.3 shows the leverage effect from Day 1 to Day 4. The leverage effect can be measured by dividing the relative change of

TABLE 5.3 Example of the Leverage Effect: A 13% Change of Stock Price Leads to 100% Change in the Option Price

	Price of Yahoo	Call Price of Yahoo
Day 1	$ 100	$ 5
Day 2	$ 105	$ 7
Day 3	$ 111	$ 9
Day 4	$ 113	$ 10
% change	13%	100%

the option price by the relative change of the underlying asset: 100%/13% = 7.69. Thus the leverage of the call on Yahoo is 7.69. This means for a change in the price of Yahoo by 1%, the call price of Yahoo will change by 7.69%.

The leverage is considered an important aspect of an option. The higher the leverage, the higher the relative profit potential. The leverage effect is generally higher the more the option is "out of the money." A call is out of the money if the strike price K is higher than the price of the underlying asset S. The higher K relative to S, the higher the leverage effect of a call. A put option is "out of the money," if the strike price K is lower than the price of the underlying asset S. The lower K relative to S, the higher the leverage effect of a put.

The leverage is an ex-post figure though, and just an estimate for the future. Furthermore, leverages are not constant. They change in time and with respect to volatility, strike, asset price, interest rate, etc. The terms "gearing" and "omega" are sometimes used as synonyms for leverage. Gearing and leverage are sometimes defined as absolute quotients (C/S), not relative quotients.

Options as a Hedging Instrument

Besides speculation, options are a great hedging tool. As mentioned in Chapter 4, hedging is entering into a second trade in order to reduce the risk of an original trade.

Let's assume an investor has bought 100 Yahoo shares at a price of $90. The investor believes Yahoo will increase, however he wants to protect his investment against a falling Yahoo price. He buys a put with a strike of $90 and pays an option premium of $5. One put on an exchange is usually denominated in 100 shares, so he pays a total of a $500 put premium. The put allows the investor to sell Yahoo (anytime during the option period if American style, only at option maturity if European style) at $90. Therefore the investor has paid a $500 "insurance premium" and has no downside price risk during the option period.

Options as an Arbitrage Instrument

Options are also used as an arbitrage instrument. Also mentioned in Chapter 4, arbitrage means profit without risk. The most popular option arbitrage is put-call parity arbitrage. It can be shown that a call plus the discounted strike price equals a put plus the stock price:

$$C + Ke^{-rT} = P + S$$

where
  C = call price
  K = strike price of call and put
  e = Euler's number, e = 2.7183...
  r = short term risk-free interest rate
  T = maturity of the call and the put
  e^{-rT} = discount factor from time T to today
  P = put price
  S = asset price

If this equation is violated, arbitrage opportunities exist. If the call has a price higher than $C = P + S - Ke^{-rT}$, the investor can sell the call, and buy the put and the underlying stock. Holding this position until option maturity will result in an arbitrage of $C - (P + S - Ke^{-rT})$.

Let's assume the call price in the market is $15, the put price is $20, the underlying stock price is $150, the strike of the call and put is $160, the risk free interest rate is 10%, and option maturity is one month. It follows that the arbitrage at option maturity T is $C - (P + S - Ke^{-rT}) = 15 - (20 + 150 - 160 \times 2.7183^{(-0.1 \times 1/12)}) = \$3.67$.

USING OPTIONS

Options on the Dow can have maturities of several hours to several years. Mostly though, options traded on financial exchanges are held for one to four weeks.

Exploiting Monthly Changes of the Dow

First, let's examine the best performing month of the Dow to determine when it is best to buy and sell options on the Dow (see Table 5.4).

TABLE 5.4 Monthly Performance of the Dow from May 30, 1968 to May 30, 1998

Month	Number of Months	Total Point Change	Average Point Change	Percentage Change
January	30	+ 1,545.20	+ 51.51	+ 19.24%
February	30	+ 1,218.42	+ 40.61	+ 15.17%
March	30	+ 497.48	+ 16.58	+ 6.19%
April	30	+ 1,096.20	+ 36.54	+ 13.65%
May	30	+1,024.10	+34.14	+12.75%
June	30	+331.50	+11.05	+4.13%
July	30	+1,099.20	+36.64	+13.69%
August	30	−387.40	−12.91	−4.82%
September	30	+143.50	+4.78	+1.79%
October	30	−651.00	−21.70	−8.10%
November	30	+1168.00	+38.93	+14.54%
December	30	+946.90	+31.56	+11.79%
Sum		+8,032.10	+267.74	+100%

Table 5.4 shows that the best performing month of the Dow is January, followed by February. August and October are the worst performing months during the last 30 years. Figure 5.8 is a graphical representation of the Dow performance, according to column 5 of Table 5.4.

The cyclical pattern in Table 5.4 and Figure 5.8 can be explained psychologically and fundamentally. In the beginning of a fiscal year traders and investors start a new era, coming back energetically and ambitiously from the Christmas holiday. This starts a high trading-volume period and, in the past, a strong upward period. The monthly increases diminish gradually until the summer and turn negative in August and October.

The poorly performing months August, September, and October can be related to deteriorating weather conditions and profit-taking by traders and investors. It seems that the wars, which have historically begun after the fall harvest, now take place at the international exchanges.

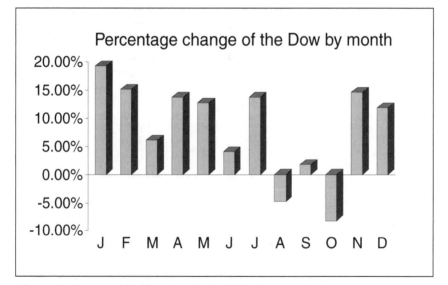

Figure 5.8   Monthly change of the Dow from May 30, 1968 to May 30, 1998 in percent of total change

The bad performance in October can also be related to *tax-loss-selling* of mutual funds. The fiscal year of mutual funds usually ends in October. Thus, at the end of October many mutual funds sell assets that they had bought at a higher price. In doing so, the mutual funds realize a loss, which they then deduct from their capital gains tax.

The well-performing months of November and December often contain a relief-rally after the weak autumn. The year-end rally in December can be partly explained by *window dressing*. Companies that close their books at the end of the year buy up the stocks they own to increase that stock price so as to show higher profits.

This established yearly trading pattern should continue into the next millennium, although of course, exceptions can occur. This leads us to Method 11.

Method 11

Buy call options on the Dow at the beginning of January to enhance profits. Buy put options on the Dow in October to hedge your portfolio.

The call option in Method 11 is bought for speculative reasons. The put in Method 11 can protect a stockholder from losing money if the market drops. For example, if the investor buys a put with a strike of 11,500 and the Dow drops to 10,500, the put holder makes $11,500 - $10,500 = $1,000. This profit compensates for potential losses in stock positions.

As explained in the beginning of this chapter, to participate strongly in the leverage effect investors should buy out of the money calls and puts. For example, if the Dow is at 10,500, buy a call with a strike of 10,700, or a put with a strike of 10,300.

As a variation to Method 11, traders can buy four-month options on the Dow in November and hold them until the end of February. Also, investors should keep in mind that the crashes in October occurred late in the month: On October 19, 1987 the Dow decreased by 15%, and on October 28, 1997 the Dow decreased by 5.8%. On the assumption that the pattern will continue, the investor would buy put options in the middle of October.

To refine Method 11, investors can look at the expense of the option. Option prices are measured in terms of implied volatility (for a detailed discussion on implied volatility, see Chapter 6). An implied volatility of 25% to 30% is considered an average price for an option. To forecast the profit outcome, we can compare the option premium with the expected monthly increase of the Dow. This brings us to Method 12.

Method 12

If the premium for a one-month at the money call is lower than the expected increase of the Dow for that period, buy the call.
As discussed previously, an at the money call has a strike price (K) which equals to the price of the underlying asset, in this case the Dow (S).

EXAMPLE OF METHOD 12
Today is January 1. The Dow is at 10,000 points. The price of a one-month call on the Dow with a strike of 10,000 (with a 27% implied volatility and a 5.13% interest rate) is $329. (All calculations are done on TRADE SMART, see www.dersoft.com. The strike and the price are quoted on the CBOE in 1/100 of the Dow. This has no effect on the result and is ignored for the sake of simplicity.)

Let's assume the Dow rises in January by 8%. (Recall that January was the month with the highest average increase of the Dow in the last 30 years; see Table 5.4.) Thus, at the end of January, the Dow is at 10,800 points. The profit from buying the call option is therefore (10,800 − 10,000) − $329 = $471. Naturally, if the investor would have bought 10 call options, the profit would be about $4,700.

Looking at the movement of the Dow in October brings us to Method 13.

Method 13

If the premium of a one-month at the money put is lower than the expected decrease of the Dow for that period, buy the put.

EXAMPLE OF METHOD 13

On October 1, the Dow is at 10,000 points. The price of a one-month put on the Dow with a strike of 10,000 (with a 27% implied volatility and a 5.13% interest rate) is $288.

Let's assume the Dow decreases in October by 6% (Recall that October was the month with the largest average decrease of the Dow in the last 30 years; see Table 5.4). Thus, at the end of October, the Dow is at 9,400 points. The profit from buying the put option is therefore (10,000 – 9,400) – $288 = $312. Naturally, if the investor would have bought 10 put options, the profit would be $3,120.

Exploiting Semi-Monthly Changes of the Dow

To further refine Methods 11 through 13, we can look at the development of the Dow within each month. Table 5.5 shows the bi-weekly performance of the Dow within each month.

In Table 5.5 we have approximated by calling Day 1 through 15 the first two weeks and Day 16 through the end of the month weeks 3 and 4.

From Table 5.5 we can see that in eight out of 12 months, the increase in the first two weeks of the month was higher than in the second half of the month. The increase in weeks 3 and 4 was only higher than the increase in weeks 1 and 2 in January, August, November, and December. If we look at the absolute changes and sum up all the increases in the first two weeks of each month (column 5), we get 73.68%.

In other words, in the last 30 years, 73.68% or 5918.05 of the 8032.10-point increase in the Dow has occurred in the first two weeks of the month. Consequently, increases for the third and fourth week equal only 26.32%, or 2114.95 points.

TABLE 5.5   Weekly Performance of the Dow from May 30, 1968 to May 30, 1998

Month	Number of Months	Total Point Change	Average Point Change	Percentage Change
January, 1 & 2 week	30	+538.70	+17.96	+6.71%
3 & 4 week		+1,006.50	+33.55	+12.53%
February, 1 & 2 week	30	+1,199.80	+37.33	+13.94%
3 & 4 week		+98.62	+3.29	+1.23%
March, 1 & 2 week	30	+799.84	+26.66	+9.96%
3 & 4 week		−302.36	−10.08	−3.76%
April, 1 & 2 week	30	+638.1	+21.27	+7.94%
3 & 4 week		+458.1	+15.27	+5.70%
May, 1 & 2 week	30	+641.4	+21.38	+7.99%
3 & 4 week		+382.7	+12.76	+4.76%
June, 1 & 2 week	30	+713.6	+23.79	+8.88%
3 & 4 week		−382.1	−12.74	−4.76%
July, 1 & 2 week	30	+684.2	+22.81	+8.52%
3 & 4 week		+415	+13.83	+5.17%
August, 1 & 2 week	30	−515.1	−17.17	−6.41%
3 & 4 week		+127.7	+4.26	+1.59%
September, 1 & 2 week	30	+407.9	+13.6	+5.08%
3 & 4 week		−264.4	−8.81	−3.29%
October, 1 & 2 week	30	+162.2	+5.41	+2.02%
3 & 4 week		−813.2	−27.11	−10.12%
November, 1 & 2 week	30	+582.2	+19.42	+7.25%
3 & 4 week		+585.3	+19.51	+7.29%
December, 1 & 2 week	30	+144.5	+4.82	+1.80%
3 & 4 week		+802.4	+26.75	+9.99%
Sum	360	+8032.10	+267.76	100.00%

It is also astonishing to see that 12.53% + 13.94% = 26.47% of the Dow increase occurred in the last two weeks of January and the first two weeks of February. This brings us to Method 14.

Method 14

If the premium of a two-week at the money call is lower than the expected increase of the Dow for that period, buy the call.

EXAMPLE OF METHOD 14

Today is February 1. The Dow stands at 10,000. A two-week call on the Dow with a strike of 9,500 (with an implied volatility of 28% and a 4.5% interest rate) costs $217.

Let's assume the Dow increases in the first two weeks of February by 8%. (Recall that the first two weeks in February have enjoyed the strongest increase in the Dow; see Table 5.5). Thus, the Dow is expected to increase to 10,000 + (10,000 × 0.08) = 10,800.

Therefore, it makes sense to buy the call, because the expected payoff of the call (10,800 − 10,000) = $800 is higher than the call premium of $217.

Looking at Table 5.5 also results in Method 15.

Method 15

If the premium of a two-week at the money put is lower than the expected decrease of the Dow for that period, buy the put.

EXAMPLE OF METHOD 15

Today is October 15. The Dow stands at 10,000. A two-week put on the Dow with a strike of 10,000 (with an implied volatility of 28% and a 4.5% interest rate) costs $199.

Let's assume the Dow decreases in the last two weeks of October by 6%. (Recall that in the last two weeks of October the Dow has typically suffered the strongest average decline; see Table 5.5.) Thus, the Dow is expected to decrease to 10,000 − (10,000 × 0.06) = 9,400.

Therefore, it makes sense to buy the put because the expected payoff of the put (10,000 – 9,400) = $600 is higher than the put premium of $199.

Keep in mind that Methods 3 through 11 are based on the historical Dow price pattern of the last 30 years. While this pattern can be psychologically and fundamentally explained, there is no guarantee of a repetition of the pattern in a specific year. Except for arbitrage, there is always risk when trading.

The January Momentum

January can be regarded as a crucial month for investing. It generates momentum in that the Dow's performance during January can act as the psychological basis for the rest of the trading year. Let's investigate the theory: *If January was an up-month, the rest of the year will be an up-year. If January was a down-month, the rest of the year will be a down-year.*

As shown in Table 5.6 and Figure 5.9, this theory has worked an astonishing 27 out of 32 years, or 84.38% of the time. The theory has even worked an astonishing 23 out of 25 years, or 92.00% in the last 25 years. The exception was 1982 and 1998. During 1982, January was negative, but then the economy turned around and came out of the recession, so the year as a whole was positive. In 1998, January was down by a mere 0.02% and the year was up by 24.74%.

Table 5.6 shows the percentage change of January and the rest of the year.

The relationship between January and the rest of the year's Dow performance is shown in the graph in Figure 5.9.

Figure 5.9 shows the reliability of the January indicator. For most years, if January was an up-month, the year as a whole was up. If January was a down-month, the year as a whole was down.

The January momentum can be used as an undercurrent for all methods suggested in this book. The bullish methods (exploiting up-movements of the Dow) should work better if January was an

TABLE 5.6 Percentage Change of the Dow in January Compared to the Rest of the Year

Year	Close at End of Year	Percentage Change in January	Percentage Change for the Whole Year
1968	943	−5.48%	+4.52
1969	800	+0.24%	−15.16
1970	838	−7.03%	+5.17
1971	890	+3.53%	+5.91
1972	1,020	+1.35%	+14.39
1973	850	−2.06%	−16.93
1974	616	+0.55%	−27.43
1975	85	+14.20%	+33.57
1976	1,004	+14.42%	+15.62
1977	831	−5.01%	−18.18
1978	805	−7.37%	−3.40
1979	838	+4.25%	+4.02
1980	964	+4.44%	+14.31
1981	875	−1.73%	−9.40
1982	1,046	−0.45%	+19.69
1983	1,258	+2.79%	+19.72
1984	1,211	−3.02%	−3.85
1985	1,546	+6.21	+26.04
1986	1,896	+1.57	+22.23
1987	1,938	+13.82	+1.98
1988	2,168	+1.00	+11.74
1989	2,753	+8.01	+24.96
1990	2,633	−5.91	−4.61
1991	3,168	+3.90	+19.55
1992	3,301	+1.72	+4.10
1993	3,754	+0.27	+13.69
1994	3,834	+5.97	+2.02
1995	5,117	+0.25	+33.37
1996	6,448	+5.44	+24.67
1997	7,908	+5.66	+21.43
1998	9,181	−0.02%	+16.10%
1999	11,452	+1.93%	+24.74%

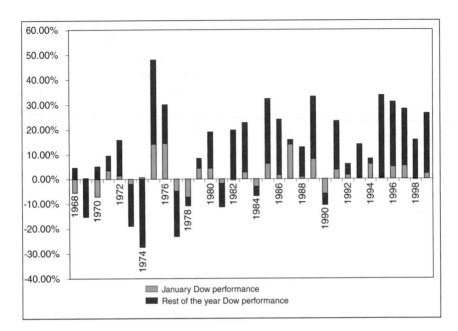

FIGURE 5.9   The January momentum

up-month. The bearish methods (exploiting down-moves in the Dow) should work better if January was a down-month.

SUMMARY

This chapter explained standard options and showed several methods that can outperform the Dow using standard options.

In most broad terms, an option is the right to do something. In finance, options are divided into calls and puts.

A call is the right, but not the obligation, to buy a certain asset at a predetermined price (strike), on a predetermined date (European style), or during a predetermined time period (American style).

A put is the right, but not the obligation, to sell a certain asset at a predetermined price (strike), on a predetermined date (European style), or during a predetermined time period (American style).

To acquire the right to buy or sell the underlying asset, the option buyer pays the option premium. Any time during the option period (if American style) the option can be exercised, i.e., the underlying asset is bought at the strike price in case of a call, or sold at the strike price in case of a put. Usually selling the option is more profitable than exercising, because the profit potential is lost when exercising prematurely.

Only the option buyer has the right to buy or sell the underlying asset. The option seller has the obligation to fulfill the trade if the option buyer decides to exercise. Thus, the difference between options and futures is that with a future, both the buyer and the seller have the obligation to trade the underlying asset. In an option, the buyer has a right, and the seller has an obligation.

As with futures, options are settled physically or in cash. Physical settlement means that the option buyer (seller) receives (delivers) the underlying asset physically in case of a call (put) and pays (receives) the strike price. All financial options, like the option on the Dow, are cash settled. Thus, the difference between the strike and the underlying asset price is credited to the option buyer, if it is positive.

Selling options is risky. The potential loss of selling a call is unlimited. The potential loss of selling a put can be high, the maximum being the strike minus the premium. The maximum loss of buying an option is limited to the option premium.

The are mainly three reasons for the popularity of options. First, options are used to speculate. Because the relative change in the option premium is usually higher than the relative change in the price of the underlying asset, options incorporate a high leverage. Options are also used to hedge (reduce risk), because they are cheap and liquid instruments. Due to a causal relationship between puts and calls known as the put-call parity, options are also used as an arbitrage instrument, which allows profit without risk.

Due to the recurring yearly pattern of the Dow, the following methods to outperform the Dow are recommended.

Because January is the best performing month over the last 30 years, buying a call on the Dow in early January is recommended. Because October is the worst performing month, with an average decrease of 8.1%, buying a put to hedge a portfolio or as a speculative position at the beginning of October is warranted.

The investor should look at the cost of the option. Options on the Dow with an implied volatility of below 25% are considered cheap. Options on the Dow with an implied volatility above 30% are considered expensive. The investor can also compare the premium of the option with the average change of the Dow, as shown in Table 5.4.

A semi-monthly analysis can refine option trading. On average, the first and second weeks of February have enjoyed the highest Dow increase, so buying a two-week call for that period is recommended. Because the third and fourth weeks of October have seen the strongest Dow decrease, buying a put for that period is recommended. The investor should look at the cost of the option and compare it with the expected change of the Dow for the relevant period.

The January momentum measures the January performance of the Dow and compares it to the yearly performance of the Dow. For the last 25 years, January was an excellent indicator for the performance of the Dow. In 23 out of the last 25 years, if the Dow was up in January, the Dow was up for the year. If the Dow was down in January, the Dow was down for the year. Therefore, the bullish methods (exploiting up-movements of the Dow) should work better if January was an up-month. The bearish methods (exploiting down-moves in the Dow) should work better if January was a down-month.

Using the suggested methods naturally assumes a repetitive investor behavior. There is ample evidence that investors repeat successful trading strategies and engage in repetitive cyclical behavior. Therefore, the suggested methods should work in the long run. Naturally, there is no guarantee that the suggested methods will work for certain specific time periods.

SUGGESTED READING

Caplan, D., (1991). *The Options Advantage: Gaining a Trading Edge Over the Markets,* (Chicago: Probus Publishing).

Chance, D. M., (1994). "Translating the Greek: The Real Meaning of Call Option Derivatives," *Financial Analysts Journal* 50 (July–August), pp. 43–49.

Cox, J. C., and M. Rubinstein, (1985). *Options Markets,* (Englewood Cliffs, NJ: Prentice-Hall).

Daigler, R. T., (1994). *Financial Futures and Options Markets: Concepts and Strategies,* (New York: HarperCollins).

Dubofsky, D. A., (1992). *Options and Financial Futures: Valuation and Uses,* (New York: McGraw-Hill).

Edwards, F. R., and C. W. Ma, (1992). *Futures and Options,* (New York: McGraw-Hill).

Fabozzi, F., ed. (1989). *The Handbook of Stock Index Futures and Options,* (Homewood, Illinois: Irwin).

Hull, J., (1995). *Introduction to Futures and Options Markets,* (Englewood Cliffs, New Jersey: Prentice-Hall).

Jarrow, R A., and S. M. Turnbull, (1996). *Derivative Securities,* (Cincinnati: South-Western).

Johnson, R. S., and C. Giaccotto, (1995). *Options and Futures: Concepts, Strategies, and Applications,* (Minneapolis: West Publishing).

Kolb, R. W., (1991). *Options: An Introduction,* (Miami: Kolb Publishing).

McMillan, L., (1993). *Options as a Strategic Investment: A Comprehensive Analysis of Listed Option Strategies,* Third Ed. (New York: New York Institute of Finance).

Meissner, G., (1998). *Trading Financial Derivatives, Futures, Swaps and Options in Theory and Application,* (New York: Simon and Schuster).

Rendleman, R., and B. Bartter, (1979). "Two State Option Pricing," *Journal of Finance,* 34, pp. 1093–1110.

Smith C. W., and C. W. Smithson, eds. (1990). *The Handbook of Financial Engineering: New Financial Product Innovations, Applications, and Analyses,* (New York: Harper Business).

Whaley, R. E., and H.R. Stoll, (1993). *Futures and Options: Theory and Applications,* (Ohio: South-Western).

Zivney, T., (1991). "The Value of Early Exercise in Option Prices: An Empirical Investigation," *Journal of Financial and Quantitative Analysis,* pp. 129–138.

6

OUTPERFORMING THE DOW USING VOLATILITY

No guts no glory: High flying stocks are volatile.

In this chapter we will utilize the different seasonal volatility patterns to outperform the Dow. Let's first take a closer look at the term volatility.

VOLATILITY—AN INTRODUCTION

The term *volatility* actually comes from volare which means "to fly." Unfortunately, that doesn't help us all that much. In financial terms, volatility is a measurement of the fluctuation-intensity of a security.

Figure 6.1 compares the price volatility of the two assets "a" and "b".

Types of Volatility

As shown in Figure 6.2, there are principally three types of volatility:

1. *Historical volatility* is the volatility that is measured from a point in time in the past until today.

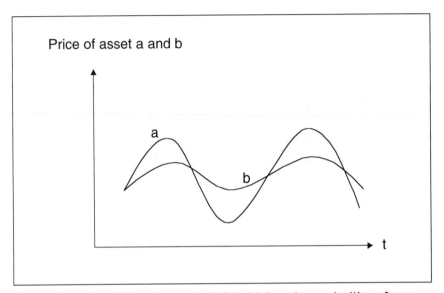

Figure 6.1   Volatility of security "a" is higher than volatility of security "b"

2. *Implied volatility* is the volatility that a trader assumes will occur from today until the maturity of the option. It is an estimation of the actual volatility. Implied volatility is the figure that is input in the option pricing formula (Black-Scholes formula) to value an option. An option that is priced with an implied volatility of around 20% can be considered

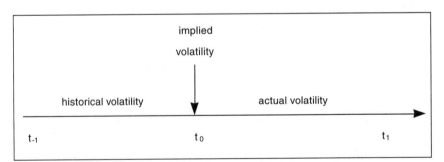

Figure 6.2   Types of volatility with respect to time

cheap. An option that is priced with a volatility of over 30% can be considered expensive.

3. *Actual volatility* is the volatility of the security that will actually occur in the future. It is an ex-ante (an expected) figure. If an option trader believes that implied volatility is smaller than actual volatility he should buy the option, and vice versa.

In trading practice, implied and historical volatility are positively correlated. Figure 6.3 shows the correlation between the implied volatility and the historical ten-day volatility of a call on the Nikkei future.

Calculation of Volatility

Volatility is calculated as the standard deviation of logarithmic price differences.

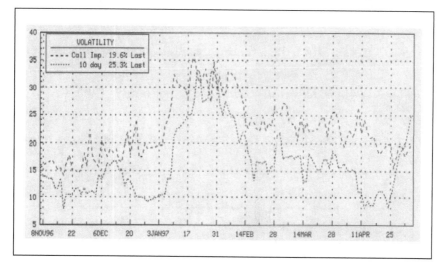

Figure 6.3 Historical and implied volatility of the Nikkei future
Source: Bloomberg Financial Systems. Used with permission from Bloomberg LLP.

Whereas the standard deviation, Std, is calculated as

$$\text{Std}(S) = \sqrt{\frac{1}{n-1} \sum_{i=1}^{n} (S_i - \bar{S})^2}$$

the volatility, Vol, is calculated as

$$\text{Vol}(S) = \sqrt{\frac{1}{n-1} \sum_{i=1}^{n} (\ln(S_i / S_{i-1}) - \bar{S}*)^2}$$

where

n = number of prices
i   = points in time
ln = natural logarithm
S_i = price at time i
$\bar{S}$ = arithmetic mean; $\bar{S} = \dfrac{1}{n} \sum_{i=1}^{n} S_i$

$\bar{S}*$ = arithmetic mean of logarithmic price differences;
$\bar{S}* = \dfrac{1}{n} \sum_{i=1}^{n} \ln(S_i / S_{i-1})$

Let's assume a stock has the prices S_i on Day 1 to Day 5 (column 2, Table 6.1). Following the standard deviation equation, the *standard deviation for a five-day stock price movement*, with a mean of $\bar{S} = \dfrac{1}{5} \sum_{i=1}^{n} S_i = \dfrac{1}{5} \times 549.28 = 109.86$ (used in column 3, Table 6.1) is:

TABLE 6.1 Deriving the Five-day Standard Deviation of a Stock Price Movement

Day i	S_i	$S_i - \bar{S}$	$(S_i - \bar{S})^2$	$\frac{1}{n-1}(S_i - \bar{S})^2$	$\sqrt{\frac{1}{n-1}(S_i - \bar{S})^2}$
1	110.24	0.38	0.1444		
2	112.18	2.32	5.3824		
3	107.35	−2.51	6.3001		
4	109.46	−0.40	0.1600		
5	110.05	0.19	0.0361		
	Σ549.28		Σ12.0230	3.0058	1.7337

Thus, the standard deviation for the five-day bond price movement is 1.7337. This means that there is a 68.27% probability (the 68.27% represents one standard deviation of the normal distribution) that the stock price the next day will be within 110.05 −/+ 1.7337, therefore between 108.32 and 111.78

Using the volatility equation, vol(s), *the daily volatility of the stock price movement* with $\overline{S}^* = \dfrac{1}{4} \sum\limits_{i=1}^{n} \ln(S_i / S_{i-1}) = \dfrac{1}{4} \times (0.017447 - 0.044060 + 0.019508 + 0.005385) = \dfrac{1}{4} \times -0.00172 = -0.00043$ (used in column 5, Table 6.2) is:

TABLE 6.2 Deriving the Five-day Volatility of a Stock Price Movement

Day$_i$	S_i	S_i/S_{i-1}	$\ln(S_i/S_{i-1})$	$\ln(S_i/S_{i-1}) - \overline{S}^*$	$(\ln(S_i/S_{i-1}) - \overline{S}^*)^2$
1	110.24				
2	112.18	1.01760	0.017447	0.017876	0.000320
3	107.35	0.95694	−0.044060	−0.04363	0.001903
4	109.46	1.01966	0.019508	0.019937	0.000397
5	110.05	1.00539	0.005385	0.005814	0.000034
			$\overline{S}^* = -0.00043$		$\Sigma = 0.002654$

Further following the volatility equation vol(s) and taking 0.002654 and multiplying it with $1/(n-1)$ ($n = 4$) yields 0.000885. Taking the square root of 0.000885 results in 0.0297 or 2.97%.

Shortcut to Calculating Volatility

There is a convenient shortcut to calculate volatility with the help of Microsoft Excel. Let's look at the same example as above: A stock price moves from 110.24 on Day 1 to 110.05 on Day 5 (see column 2 in Table 6.3). We then calculate the quotient of the stock price and

TABLE 6.3 Using Excel's "Stdev" Function to Calculate the Five-day Volatility of a Stock Price Movement

Day i	S_i	S_i/S_{i-1}	$\ln(S_i/S_{i-1})$	Using Excel's "Stdev" Function
1	110.24			
2	112.18	1.01760	0.017447	
3	107.35	0.95694	−0.044060	
4	109.46	1.01966	0.019508	
5	110.05	1.00539	0.005385	
				=Stdev (0.017447, −0.044060, 0.019508 0.005385) = **2.97%**

the stock price the day before and the natural logarithm, as in Table 6.2.

Since volatility is the standard deviation of these relative daily differences, we now use Excel's standard deviation function "Stdev" on the values 0.017447, −0.04406, 0.019508, and 0.005385. We then get the same result as in Table 6.2: 0.0297 or 2.97% daily volatility.

Interpretation of the Result

The daily volatility of the stock price is 2.97%. This means that there is a 68.27% probability (the 68.27% represents one standard deviation of a normal distribution) that the stock price the next day will be within 110.05 (today's value) −/+ 2.97% × 110.05, therefore, between 106.78 and 113.32.

Furthermore, there is a 95.45% probability (95.45% represents two standard deviations of the normal distribution) that the stock price the next day will be within 110.05 −/+ 110.05 × 2 × 2.97%, therefore, between 103.51 and 116.59.

Also, there is a 99.73% probability (99.73% represents three standard deviations of the normal distribution) that the stock price the next day will be within 110.05 –/+ 110.05 × 3 × 2.97%, therefore, between 100.24 and 119.86.

To *annualize* the volatility, the calculated volatility has to be multiplied by the square root of the observation frequency. In the above example, we have daily data. There are roughly 252 trading days in a year. Thus, the annualized volatility is 2.97% × $\sqrt{252}$ = 47.15%. Thus, there is a 68.27% probability that the price of the stock within the next year will be 110.05 –/+ 0.4715 × 110.05, so between 57.16 and 161.94.

Features of the Volatility Concept

The fact that the financial markets use volatility and not the standard deviation to determine and compare the fluctuation intensity of securities is sensible: Stock prices moving 1, 2, 3 and 1001, 1002, 1003 lead to the same standard deviation of 1, although the *relative* price fluctuation of 1, 2, 3 is much higher than a stock price movement of 1001, 1002, 1003. The volatility concept reflects this *relative* difference in the fluctuation. The volatility of a stock moving 1, 2, 3 is 20.34%, the volatility of a stock moving 1001, 1002, 1003 is close to zero.

The volatility concept is a "trend concept": If the price of a security increases with the same constant rate, e.g., 10%: 100, 110, 121, 133.1, 146.41 and so on, it follows that the volatility is zero. The volatility is zero for *any* constant rate of growth of a security. (The doubtful reader might want to do the calculations in order to confirm this.)

The reason for the zero volatility is the fact that in an arbitrage free market, all securities have to grow with the risk-free interest rate. Arbitrage occurs if an asset grows by more or less than the risk-free interest rate. An investor would buy the security with the higher return and sell the security with the lower return.

Armed with knowledge about options and volatility, we can now look at methods to beat the Dow using volatility.

USING VOLATILITY

Empirical Volatility Data

Table 6.4 summarizes the volatility of the Dow for the last 30 years. Column 3 shows the average monthly volatilities. Multiplying column 3 with the square root of the months in a year, (i.e., with $\sqrt{12}$) we get the average monthly annualized Dow volatility in column 4. Column 4 shows that the lowest volatility of the Dow is in June with 11.91% and the highest volatility is in October with 17.94%. Figure 6.4 gives a graphical representation of Table 6.4.

Table 6.4 and Figure 6.4 lead us to Method 16.

Method 16

Buy a one-month straddle (see Figure 5.5) at the beginning of the volatile month of October.

TABLE 6.4   Monthly Volatilities of the Dow

	Observed Number of Months	Average Monthly Volatility	Average Monthly Annualized Volatility
January	30	4.12%	14.29%
February	30	3.80%	13.18%
March	30	3.80%	13.18%
April	30	3.94%	13.65%
May	30	3.80%	13.18%
June	30	**3.44%**	**11.91%**
July	30	3.53%	12.22%
August	30	3.90%	13.49%
September	30	3.76%	13.02%
October	30	**5.18%**	**17.94%**
November	30	4.17%	14.45%
December	30	**3.80%**	**13.18%**
Average		3.94%	13.65%

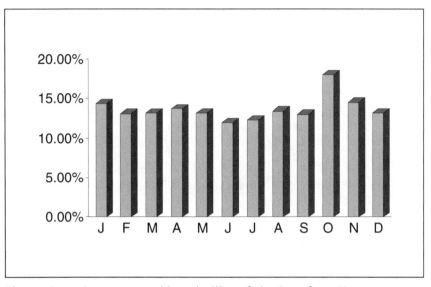

Figure 6.4 Average monthly volatility of the Dow from May 30, 1968 to May 30, 1998

From our earlier analysis in Table 5.4, we saw that the Dow, on average, decreased in October over the last 30 years. However, in 1993 and 1996 the Dow had strong gains in October, so Method 16 is justified.

When using Method 16, an investor should inquire as to the expense of the straddle. As explained earlier in this chapter, the expense of an option is measured by the implied volatility. An option that is priced with an implied volatility of around 20% can be considered cheap. An option that is priced with an implied volatility of over 30% can be considered expensive.

Investors can also quite easily find out the implied volatility of an option on their own. Many cheap and easy-to-use option pricing packages are available. (See for example www.dersoft.com.)

EXAMPLE OF METHOD 16

Today is October 1. The Dow stands at 11,000. An investor buys a one-month straddle (= a call and a put) on the Dow. The strad-

*dle with a strike of 11,000 (and with an implied volatility of 20%
and a 4.5% interest rate) costs $503.*

*The average expected volatility for October is 5.18%. (see
Table 6.3) This means that there is a 95.45% probability that the
Dow in October will be between 11,000 −/+ 11,000 ×2 ×0.0518,
so between 9,861 and 12,139.*

*Let's assume the Dow decreases to 10.140. Thus, the call
expires worthless. However, the profit on the put is (11,000 −
10,140 = $860.*

*Thus, the overall profit from buying the straddle is $860 −
$503 = $357. Naturally, if the investor would have bought 10
straddles, the profit would have been $3,570.*

Method 17

*Sell a one-month straddle (see Figure 5.5) at the beginning of the
low volatility month of June. Be sure to have a stop.*

Using Method 17 an investor can exploit the low volatility of
the month of June by selling a straddle. As in Method 16, the
investor should know the implied volatility that is used to price the
straddle. Again, an option that is priced with an implied volatility
of around 20% can be considered cheap. An option that is priced
with a volatility of over 30% can be considered expensive.

*It is very important that the investor has a stop when using
Method 17.* As discussed in Chapter 5, selling options is dangerous
because of the high potential loss. Selling a call can lead to unlimited losses. Selling a put can lead to high losses, the maximum
being the strike price minus the option premium. Therefore, the
investor should have a certain predetermined loss-level (stop), at
which he or she reverses the short straddle trade to prevent higher
potential losses.

EXAMPLE OF METHOD 17
*Today is June 1. The Dow stands at 11,000. An investor sells a
one-month straddle (= a call and a put) on the Dow. The straddle, with a strike of 11,000 (and with an implied volatility of
27% and a 4.5% interest rate), costs $678.*

*The average expected monthly volatility for June is 3.44%
(see Table 6.3). This means that there is a 95.45% probability
that the Dow in June will be between 11,000 −/+ 11,000 × 2 ×
0.0344, so between 10,244 and 11.756.*

*Let's assume the Dow decreases to 10.400. Thus, the sold call
expires worthless. However, on the sold put the loss is (11,000 −
10.400) = $600.*

*Thus, the overall profit from selling the straddle is $678 −
$600 = $78. Naturally, if the investor would have sold 10 straddles, the profit would have been $780.*

The stop that the investor sets to prevent potential losses can
be 10,321 (= 11,000 − 678) and 11,678 (= 11,000 + 678). At these levels the investor can then buy back the straddle. If the market drops
further than 10,321, the investor would lose money because the
sold put would get deeper in the money. If the market rises above
11,678 the investor would lose money because the sold call would
get deeper in the money.

To refine Methods 16 and 17, we can look at volatility data on
a semi-monthly basis. Doing so yields the data in Table 6.5.

From Table 6.5, we derive Method 18.

Method 18

*Buy a two-week straddle (see Figure 5.5) at the beginning of the
third week of October.*

Method 18 exploits the high volatility of late October. As in
Methods 16 and 17, investors should ask a broker about the cost of
the straddle. A more interested investor can determine the implied
volatility by himself. Either he can write his own Black-Scholes
pricing model or buy reasonably priced option software (see
www.dersoft.com). Remember, implied volatility of around 20% can
be considered cheap and implied volatility of over 30% can be considered expensive.

EXAMPLE OF METHOD 18

*Today is October 14. The Dow stands at 11,000. An investor
buys a two-week straddle (buys a call and a put) on the Dow.*

TABLE 6.5 Semi-monthly Volatilities of the Dow

	Observed Number of Months	Average Monthly Volatility	Average Monthly Annualized Volatility
January, 1 & 2 week	30	2.94%	14.73%
3 & 4 week		2.69%	13.53%
February, 1 & 2 week	30	2.50%	12.57%
3 & 4 week		2.62%	13.25%
March, 1 & 2 week	30	2.47%	12.37%
3 & 4 week		2.69%	13.42%
April, 1 & 2 week	30	2.75%	13.89%
3 & 4 week		2.59%	12.98%
May, 1 & 2 week	30	2.47%	12.35%
3 & 4 week		2.72%	13.63%
June, 1 & 2 week	30	**2.28%**	11.49%
3 & 4 week		2.40%	12.00%
July, 1 & 2 week	30	2.43%	12.19%
3 & 4 week		2.37%	11.85%
August, 1 & 2 week	30	2.50%	12.48%
3 & 4 week		2.72%	13.61%
September, 1 & 2 week	30	2.66%	13.36%
3 & 4 week		2.43%	12.21%
October, 1 & 2 week	30	3.04%	15.31%
3 & 4 week		**3.73%**	18.76%
November, 1 & 2 week	30	2.88%	14.45%
3 & 4 week		2.88%	14.39%
December, 1 & 2 week	30	2.62%	13.13%
3 & 4 week		2.47%	12.45%
Average		2.66%	13.35%

The straddle with a strike of 11,000 (and with an implied volatility of 20% and a 4.5% interest rate) costs $355.

The average expected volatility for the last two weeks of October is 3.73% (see Table 6.5). This means that there is a 95.45% probability that the Dow in the last two weeks of Octo-

ber will be between 11,000 –/+ 11,000 × 2 × 0.0373, so between 10,179 and 11.821.

Let's assume the Dow decreases to 10,500. Thus, the call expires worthless. However, the profit on the put is 11,000 – 10,500 = \$500.

Thus, the overall profit from buying the straddle is \$500 – 355 = \$145.

From Table 6.5 we also derive Method 19.

Method 19

Sell a two-week straddle (see Figure 5.6) at the beginning of June. Be sure to have a stop.

Method 19 exploits the usually low volatility of the first two weeks of June. Again, as with Methods 16 through 18, the investor should pay attention to the implied volatility. Below 25% implied volatility, an option is considered cheap, above 30% options are considered expensive.

As in Method 17, the investor should have a stop. If the market unexpectedly becomes volatile and losses occur, the investor should have a predetermined level at which he reverses the trade and cuts his losses.

EXAMPLE OF METHOD 19

Today is June 1. The Dow stands at 11,000. An investor sells a two-week straddle (sells a call and a put) on the Dow. The straddle with a strike of 11,000 (and with an implied volatility of 25% and a 4.5% interest rate) costs \$444.

The average expected volatility for the first two weeks of June is 2.28% (see Table 6.4). This means that there is a 95.45% probability that the Dow in the first two weeks of June will be between 11,000 –/+ 11,000 × 2 × 0,0228, so between 10,498 and 11,502.

Let's assume the Dow decreases to 10,700. Thus, the sold call expires worthless. However, on the sold put the loss is (11,000 – 10,700) = \$300.

Thus, the overall profit from selling the straddle is $444 – $300 = $144.

The stop that the investor sets to prevent potential losses can be at 10,556 = 11,000 – (444) and 11,444 (= 11,000 + 444). At these levels the investor can buy back the straddle. If the market drops further than 10,556 the investor would lose money because the sold put would get deeper in the money. If the market rises above 11,444 the investor would lose money because the call would get deeper in the money.

Another way to achieve high profits is by using the *covered call writing* strategy, explained in Figure 5.7. The covered call writing strategy works very well with high-tech stocks because these stocks have a high actual volatility. The high actual volatility translates into a high implied volatility, as was shown in Figure 6.3. A high implied volatility is the same as a high option price. These high option prices can be exploited by selling the option. However, because option selling is risky, we have to hedge. In the case of covered call writing, the hedge is owning the underlying stock. Since the implied volatility is usually highest for short-term options, a monthly covered call writing strategy is warranted.

This brings us to Method 20.

Method 20

Sell consecutive one-month at the money calls on a high volatility high-tech stocks, which you own (known as covered call writing strategy).

Let's look at an example of Method 20.

EXAMPLE OF METHOD 20

It is June 16. An investor owns 100 Yahoo shares. Yahoo trades at $150. The market is going sideways. The investor wants to increase her Yahoo return and sells one call on Yahoo with a strike of 150. The call expires on the third Friday of July, which *is July 16. The implied market volatility of a one-month Yahoo call is 80%.*

The call premium, with a one-month interest rate of 4%, is $13.92. (All calculations are done on TRADE SMART, see *www.dersoft.com,* page 2.) *Thus, the amount the investor receives is $13.92 × 100 shares = $1,392. If the investor uses this strategy for 12 months, her enhanced Yahoo return is $1,392 * 12 = $16,704. Therefore, the return on the $15,000 value of Yahoo shares is $16,704 / $15,000 = 111.36%!*

Where is the catch of Method 20? There are two risks involved:

If the Yahoo stock price keeps rising, the Yahoo shares will be called (the call is exercised) and the investor will have to buy back Yahoo at the higher price. In other words, with this example of method 20, the investor caps her Yahoo profits at a Yahoo price of the strike price plus the premium, $150 + $13.92 = $163.92.

Since the investor owns the Yahoo stock, another risk of Method 20 is that Yahoo might drop sharply. However, if the investor keeps selling calls on Yahoo, the decrease can be compensated for by the option premiums she receives.

Altogether, the covered call writing strategy on highly volatile stocks, such as high-tech stocks, is a great and widely used opportunity to increase returns.

SUMMARY

This chapter explained the concept of volatility and several methods to beat the Dow using volatility were shown.

Volatility measures the degree of fluctuation of a security or an index. There are three main types of volatility. The historical volatility measures the past fluctuation of a security. Implied volatility is an estimate of the actual volatility that will occur from today until the maturity of the option. Implied volatility is the number that is input in the option pricing formula (Black-Scholes formula) to value an option. Actual volatility is the volatility of the security that will actually occur from today until option maturity.

Volatility measures the relative change of a security. The concept of volatility is superior to the concept of standard deviation, which measures the absolute change of a security. Volatility is a "trend concept": If a stock increases or decreases with a constant rate, e.g., 10%, it follows that the volatility of the stock is zero.

October has been the month with the highest volatility in the last 30 years. Therefore, buying a one-month straddle at the beginning of October is recommended. June has been the month with the lowest volatility in the last 30 years. Therefore, selling a one-month straddle at the beginning of June is warranted. Because selling options is risky, the investor should have a stop when selling a straddle.

A semi-monthly analysis can refine these methods. The highest volatility has occurred in the last two weeks of October. Therefore buying, a two-week straddle in the middle of October is recommended. The lowest volatility has occurred in the first two weeks of June. Therefore, selling a two-week straddle at the beginning of June seems warranted. Again, the investor should have a stop when selling a straddle.

When trading straddles, an investor should check the price of the considered calls and puts. Calls and puts priced with lower than 25% implied volatility are considered cheap, options with an implied volatility above 30% are considered expensive.

Among the most popular option strategies is the covered call writing strategy. It consists of selling a call on a stock that is owned. High-tech stocks are among the most volatile stocks, so calls on high-tech stocks are the most expensive. Therefore, the covered call writing strategy is most effective on highly volatile high-tech stocks. The return of the covered call writing strategy can be higher than 100%, due to the high premium of calls on high-tech stocks.

There are two possible drawbacks to covered call writing: If the underlying stock drops sharply, the investor will lose money because the stock is owned. If the underlying stock increases sharply, the stock will be called and the investor will not participate in the stock price increase. Therefore, a covered call writing strategy is recommended in a sideways market.

As in Chapters 3 through 5, the methods in Chapter 6 were based on repetitive investor behavior. There is ample evidence that investors repeat successful trading strategies and engage in repetitive cyclical behavior. Therefore, the suggested methods should work in the long run. However, be aware that there is no guarantee that the suggested methods will work for certain specific time periods.

SUGGESTED READING

Amin, K., and A. Morton, (1994). "Implied Volatility Functions in Arbitrage-Free Term Structure Models," *Journal of Financial Economics,* 35, pp. 141–80.

Bollerslev T., R. Chou, and K. Kroner, (1992). "ARCH modeling in finance," *Journal of Econometrics,* 52, pp. 5–59.

Cox, J. C., and M. Rubinstein, (1985). *Options Markets,* (Englewood Cliffs, NJ: Prentice-Hall).

Fabozzi, F., ed., (1989). *The Handbook of Stock Index Futures and Options,* (Homewood, Illinois: Irwin).

Hull, J., (1997). *Options, Futures and Other Derivatives,* (Englewood Cliffs, NJ: Prentice-Hall).

Kolb, R. W., (1991). *Options: An Introduction,* (Miami: Kolb Publishing).

Longstaff, F. A., and E. S. Schwartz, (1992). "Interest Rate Volatility and the Term Structure: A Two Factor General Equilibrium Model," *Journal of Finance,* 47(4), pp. 1259–82.

Meissner, G., (1998). *Trading Financial Derivatives; Futures, Swaps and Options in Theory and Application,* (New York: Simon and Schuster).

Meissner, G., (1999). "Volatility Arbitrage in Fixed Income Markets," *Derivatives Quarterly,* 5(3).

Nelson, D., (1991). "Conditional Heteroskedasticity in Asset Returns: A New Approach," *Econometrica,* 59(2).

Spinner, K., (1997). "Estimating Volatility," *Derivatives Strategy.* Also on www.derivatives.com/archives/1997/0397fea2.thml

Whaley, R. E., and H. R. Stoll, (1993). *Futures and Options: Theory and Applications,* (Ohio: South-Western, Publishing Co.).

7

OUTPERFORMING THE DOW USING EXOTIC OPTIONS

---

*Far too many notes, my dear Mozart, far too
complicated.*
—Ferdinand of Austria to Wolfgang Amadeus Mozart

Exotic options are options whose payoff, valuation, and hedging
procedures are different, usually more complicated than those of
standard options. Exotic options have become increasingly popular
in the recent past. The reason is that many exotics can precisely
replicate an investor's view about market movements. Also some
exotics, e.g., average options, are cheaper than standard options,
and are therefore more attractive to investors. Most exotic options
can be traded on the CBOE (Chicago Board of Option Exchange),
where they are called "Flex Options," or they may be traded
directly with an investment bank.

The main reason for the use of exotic options in the financial
markets is *speculation.* Some exotics, however, are utilized for
hedging purposes (quantos, average options).

In this chapter, we will categorize the standard exotic options into seven groups:

- Digital options
- Barrier options
- Lookback options
- Average options
- Compound options
- Multi-asset or correlation options
- Hybrids

DIGITAL OPTIONS

A *digital option* is an option that pays a fixed amount of cash if the option finishes in the money. The cash amount is paid regardless of how deep the option finishes in the money.

The nature of a digital option is close to that of a standard bet. If an investor believes that at a certain date the Dow will be above or below a strike K, then he can enter into a bet. If the investor is correct, he receives a certain amount of cash. If he is incorrect, he receives nothing and his loss is equal to the originally paid option premium. Therefore, digital options are also called binary or bet options.

As in a standard option, digital options are divided into calls and puts:

Digital Calls

The payoff of a digital call looks like Figure 7.1. As shown in Figure 7.1, the payoff (option value at option maturity) of a digital call is discontinuous. If the Dow at option maturity is above the strike K, the option is in the money and the option buyer receives the agreed amount of cash "0b". Thus, the overall profit of the investor is the amount "0b" minus the premium paid at option start "0a". Naturally, the option premium "0a" is lower than the

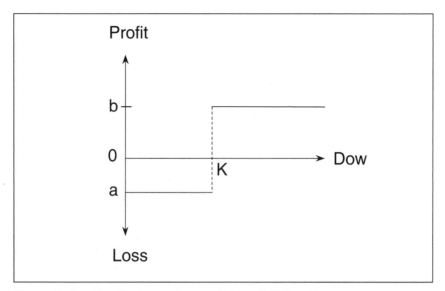

Figure 7.1 Payoff of a cash or nothing digital call

agreed upon cash "0b". Otherwise the option buyer cannot make money (because the option premium "0a" was paid at the option start date).

If the Dow at option maturity is lower than K, the option is out of the money and the option buyer loses the premium "Oa".

The reader should compare the payoff of a digital call (Figure 7.1) with the payoff of a standard call (Figure 5.1). The main difference between the two options is that the cash or nothing call buyer is indifferent to *how much* the option finishes in the money. As long as it finishes a little in the money, the maximum profit of "Ob" is achieved. Thus, the digital call is advantageous compared to a standard call as long as the Dow finishes just slightly above the strike K. This brings us to Method 21.

Method 21

Buy a cash or nothing call if you believe that at option maturity, the Dow will be just slightly above the strike K.

Digital Puts

An investor who has no clear view on the price movement of a stock or the Dow, but believes the Dow will be lower than a certain strike price, can buy a digital put.

As in Figure 7.1, the payoff (the option value at option maturity) of a digital put in Figure 7.2 is discontinuous. If the Dow at option maturity is below the strike K, the option is in the money and the option buyer receives the agreed amount of cash "Ob". Thus, the overall profit of the investor is the amount "Ob" minus the premium, paid at option start, "Oa". Naturally, the option premium "Oa" is lower than the agreed upon cash "Ob". Otherwise the option buyer cannot make money (because the option premium "Oa" was paid at the option start date).

If the Dow at option maturity is higher than K, the option is out of the money and the option buyer loses the premium "Oa". Comparing the payoff of a digital put (Figure 7.2) with that of a standard put (Figure 5.3), we can see that the digital put is

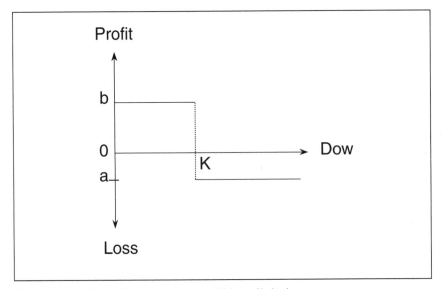

Figure 7.2   Payoff of a cash or nothing digital put

advantageous if the Dow is just slightly lower than the strike K. This brings us to Method 22.

Method 22

Buy a cash or nothing put if you believe that at option maturity the Dow will be just slightly lower than the strike K.

CONTINGENT PREMIUM OPTION

There are several types of options that are derived by combinations of digital options and standard options. One of the most famous is the *contingent premium option*. It is one of the very few options where the premium is conditional. A contingent premium option is an option where the option buyer pays the option premium at option maturity, but only if the option finishes in the money. The option buyer has to exercise the option if it finishes in the money.

The option seller makes money if the contingent option finishes in the money by a small amount, i.e., if the Dow is between K and S_1 (see Figure 7.3).

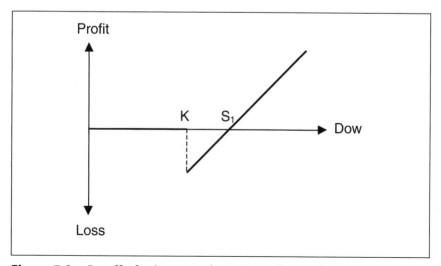

Figure 7.3 Payoff of a long contingent premium call

The payoff of a contingent premium call can be replicated by adding the payoff of a standard long call (Figure 5.1) and a digital put (Figure 7.2) with the same strike and maturity.

Because the option premium is only paid if the option finishes in the money, contingent premium options have high customer appeal. However, the price of an at the money contingent option (Dow price equals strike price) is about twice as high as the price of a standard at the money option. This naturally reduces the demand for contingent premium options. Nevertheless, consider Method 23.

Method 23

If you believe the Dow will finish above S_1, may finish below K, and is not likely to finish between K and S_1, enter into a contingent premium option with strike K.

BARRIER OPTIONS

If you're down and out...

One of the most popular exotic options is the *barrier option*. Barrier options are cheaper than standard options, and can precisely replicate an investor's view on the Dow. A barrier option is an option whose payoff depends not only on the price of Dow at maturity, but also on whether the Dow reaches a predefined barrier during the option period. This is the definition for an *inside* barrier, where the Dow itself determines the barrier level and the payoff at maturity. For example, a call on the Dow is knocked out if the Dow breaches the level of 11,000. In an *outside* barrier, *two* assets are involved. One asset is the underlying asset determining the payoff, the other asset determines the barrier level, e.g., a call on the Dow will be knocked out if the dollar breaches 1.70 against the Deutsch Mark.

In the following section we will focus on inside barriers. Furthermore, we will discuss European style barrier options, which can only be exercised at option maturity.

Barrier options are the most popular exotic options and trade frequently, especially in the foreign exchange market.

There are two basic types of barrier options:

- Knock-in barrier options
- Knock-out barrier options

A *knock-in barrier option* is an option that is "knocked in" (starts existing) if the underlying asset touches or breaks a predefined level. This level is called *knock-in strike KI*.

A *knock-out barrier option* is an option that is "knocked out" (stops existing) if the underlying asset touches or breaks a predefined level. This level is called *knock-out strike KO*.

Because knock-in options sometimes do not get knocked in and knock-out options can be knocked out, barrier options are *cheaper* than standard options. This is the main reason for their popularity.

A very important feature of a barrier option is the leverage effect, as discussed in Chapter 5 (see Table 5.3). Most barrier options have a higher leverage, and thus a higher relative profit potential than standard options.

Other Types of Barrier Options

Combining calls and puts with knock-in and knock-out features, eight types of barrier options result. The four call types are:

Up-and-in call (C_{ui})

Up-and-out call (C_{uo})

Down-and-in call (C_{di})

Down-and-out call (C_{do})

The four put types are:

Up-and-in put (P_{ui})

Up-and-out put (P_{uo})·

Down-and-in put (P_{di})

Down-and-out put (P_{do})

Let's look at the four call types in more detail.

Up-and-In Call   An up-and-in call starts existing when the Dow reaches a certain knock-in strike level. If the Dow reaches or breaks that level, the up-and-in call becomes a standard call option.

Thus, the payoff of an up-and-in call is that of a regular call, max [0, S_T – K], if the underlying price S is at or above the knock-in strike KI at least once during the option period. If S < KI during the entire option period, the option is not knocked in and no payoff for the option buyer occurs.

The strike K has to be set lower than the knock-in strike KI, otherwise the option would be a standard call option right from the start. Figure 7.4 shows an up-and-in call, that is not knocked in,

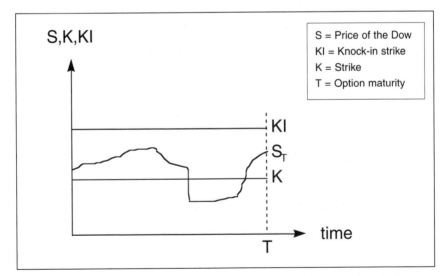

Figure 7.4   An up-and-in call not being knocked in, so the payoff of a standard call S_T – K does not occur

because during the option period the Dow price S is always lower than the knock-in strike KI.

From Figure 7.4, we derive Method 24.

Method 24

Buy a cheap and highly leveraged up-and-in call if you are very bullish and believe that the Dow will reach or go higher than the knock-in level KI at least once during the option period.

Up and Out Call   The payoff of an up-and-out call is that of a regular call if, during the option period, the Dow price S is never at or above the knock-out strike KO. If, however, the underlying price touches or goes above the knock-out strike, the option stops existing (see Figure 7.5).

Naturally, at option start, the Dow price S_0 has to be lower than the knock-out strike KO. Otherwise, the option wouldn't even start

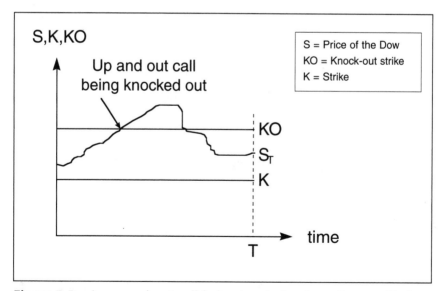

Figure 7.5 An up-and-out call being knocked out, so the payoff of a standard call $S_T - K$ does not occur

existing. Furthermore, the strike K has to be lower than the knock-out strike KO. Otherwise, the option can never finish in the money. This leads us to Method 25.

Method 25

Buy a cheap and highly leveraged up-and-out call if you are bullish on the Dow, but believe that the Dow will never be equal or higher than the knock-out strike KO during the option period.

Down-and-In Call   The payoff of a down-and-in call will occur if the Dow price S is at or below the knock-in strike at least once during the option period. The payoff is 0 if the Dow stays above the knock-in strike KI during the entire option period. At option start, the Dow price S_0 is higher than the knock-in strike KI. Otherwise, the option would be knocked in right at the start and will equal a standard call (see Figure 7.6).

Figure 7.6 leads us to Method 26.

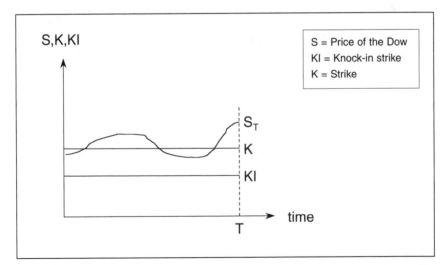

Figure 7.6 A down-and-in call never being knocked in, so the payoff of a standard call $S_T - K$ does not occur

Method 26

Buy a cheap and highly leveraged down-and-in call if you are bullish on the Dow, but believe the Dow will be at or lower than the knock-out strike KI at least once during the option period.

Down-and-Out Call   Finally, let's look at a down-and-out call in detail. The payoff of a down-and-out call is that of a regular call if, during the option period, the Dow price S is always above the knock-out strike KO.

The payoff is zero if at least once during the option period the Dow price S is at or below the knock-out strike.

Naturally, at option start the Dow price S_0 has to be higher than the knock-out strike KO. Otherwise, the option would get knocked out the moment it started (not a great prospect for the option buyer) (see Figure 7.7).

Figure 7.7 leads us to Method 27.

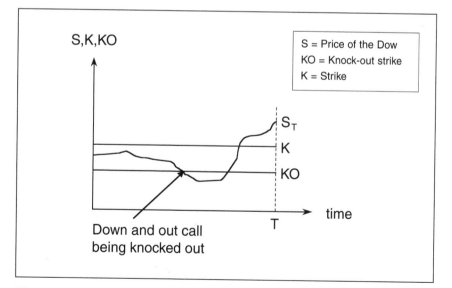

Figure 7.7   A down-and-out call being knocked out, so the payoff of a standard call $S_T - K$ does not occur

Method 27

Buy a cheap and highly leveraged down-and-out call if you are bull-ish on the Dow and don't believe that the Dow will be at or lower than the knock-out strike KO during the option period.

The same basic logic that applies to barrier call options also applies to barrier put options:

- An up-and-in put should be purchased if the investor believes in a decreasing Dow, but believes that the Dow will be at or higher than the knock-in level KI at least once during the option period.
- An up-and-out put should be purchased if the investor believes that the Dow will decrease, and the Dow will never be at or higher than the knock-out level KO.
- A down-and-in put should be purchased if the investor believes the Dow will decrease sharply, even be at or below the knock-in level KI at least once during the option period.
- A down-and-out put should be purchased if the investor believes that the Dow will decrease, but will never be at or fall below the knock-out level KO during the option period.

Advantages of Barrier Options

As already mentioned, the advantage of barrier options is that they are cheaper than standard options and usually have a higher lever-age. High leverage means a high relative change of the option price in relation to a relative change of the Dow.

George Soros bought cheap, highly leveraged down-and-in puts when the pound sterling abandoned the European rate mechanism in September 1992 and devalued strongly. He made tons of money.

Barrier options can also serve as a cheaper hedge than stan-dard options. An investor who wants to hedge a long position in the Dow can buy a cheap up-and-out put. The risk is that the market goes up first, so the up-and-out put gets knocked out. If the market then decreases, the investor is left without the put as a hedge.

Also, an investor who is long the Dow and believes the market might drop, but not significantly, can buy a cheap down-and-out put as a hedge. This strategy is also risky though. If the market does drop sharply, the put gets knocked out and the investor is left un-hedged.

Disadvantage of Barrier Options

Naturally, the disadvantage of barrier options is that an investor will not receive his payoff at option maturity, since the option has never been knocked in or has been knocked out. Investors in barrier options should be aware of this drawback.

The selling of barrier options is not recommended because of the high potential loss. Except for the up-and-out call, the maximum loss of barrier calls is unlimited. The maximum loss for barrier puts is not unlimited, but can take values up to the strike price K.

For an investment bank that is usually the seller of barrier options, the pricing of barriers is quite straightforward (barrier option pricing models can be found at www.dersoft.com). However, the hedging of the various risks of barrier options can be quite difficult.

Variations of Barrier Options

There are numerous variations of barrier options traded in the market. The most popular types are:

- *Rebate barrier option:* In a rebate barrier option, a certain amount of cash is paid if the option is knocked out to make the knocked out option holder feel a little better.
- *Multi-barrier option:* An option that has several knock-in and/or knock-out barriers for different time periods.
- *Ratchet option:* An option where gains are locked in if the underlying price reaches certain levels. If the ratchet

approaches infinity, the ratchet option becomes a lookback option (explained in the next section).

- *Shout option or deferred strike option:* An option where the buyer can determine the strike at any point in time. The strike is equal to, or stands in some relation to, the underlying price at the time of the shouting.

- *Ladder option, cliquet option, or reset option:* An option where the strike is reset periodically if the underlying price reaches certain barriers. The barriers can be determined numerically or at certain points in time.

- *One touch option or forced exercise option:* An option that is automatically exercised if the underlying price reaches a certain barrier.

- *Partial barriers:* A barrier option that is only knocked out or in for a certain time period or for a certain amount.

- *Outside barrier option:* As already mentioned, an option where the asset that determines the barrier (i.e., the dollar in exchange rate) is different from the underlying asset (i.e., IBM).

- *Teaser option:* An option where the knocked out buyer when being knocked out, is forced to buy another knock-out option.

- *Combinations:* Naturally, all types of barrier options can be combined to create an option that exactly replicates an investor's view of the market.

LOOKBACK OPTIONS

Don't look back in anger.

Lookback options allow the buyer to buy the Dow at the lowest level or sell it at the highest level that the Dow reaches during the option period.

There are two basic types of European lookback options:

In a lookback *strike* option, no constant strike is set at the trade date. The strike is the lowest (S_{min}) or highest (S_{max}) level that the Dow reaches during the option period.

The payoff of a lookback strike *call* on the Dow is the difference between the price of the Dow at option maturity S_T and the minimum of the Dow during the option period S_{min}:

$$S_T - S_{min}$$

The payoff of a lookback strike *put* on the Dow is the difference between the highest price of the Dow during the option period S_{max} and the price of the Dow at option maturity S_T:

$$S_{max} - S_T$$

Note that the payoff of a lookback strike option is by definition greater or equal to zero (see Figure 7.8).

An investor who buys lookback strike options should have Dow expectations such as Methods 28 and 29.

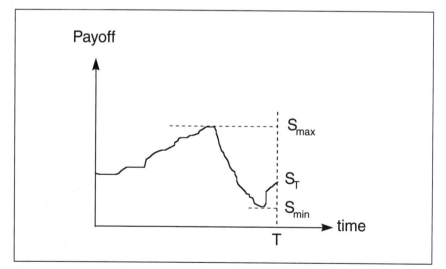

Figure 7.8 Payoff of a lookback strike call $S_T - S_{min}$; payoff of a lookback strike put $S_{max} - S_T$

Method 28

Buy a lookback strike call if you believe the Dow will first drop and then rise sharply.

Method 29

Buy a lookback strike put if you believe the Dow will first rise and then drop sharply.

The selling of a lookback option is not recommended, because of the high loss potential. The maximum loss of a lookback strike call is theoretically unlimited.

In a lookback *price* option a strike K is defined at the trade date, as in a standard option. The payoff at option maturity is the difference between that strike K and the maximum or the minimum of the underlying price during the option period.

The payoff of a lookback price *call* on the Dow is the difference between the highest price of the Dow during the option period S_{max} and the strike K, or zero:

$$\max (S_{max} - K, 0)$$

The payoff of a lookback price *put* on the Dow is the difference between the strike K and the lowest price of the Dow during the option period S_{min}, or zero (see Figure 7.9):

$$\max (K - S_{min}, 0)$$

An investor who buys lookback strike options should have the following Dow expectation. If daily (closing) prices are used to determine S_{max} and S_{min}, Methods 30 and 31 apply.

Method 30

Buy a lookback price call if you believe the Dow will rise sharply at least one day during the option period.

Method 31

Buy a lookback price put if you believe the Dow will fall sharply at least one day during the option period.

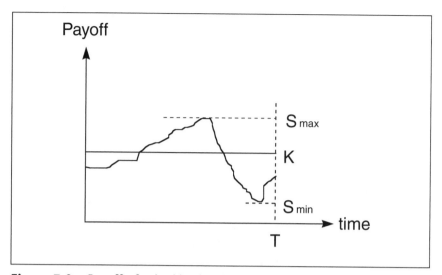

Figure 7.9   Payoff of a lookback price call S_{max} – K; payoff of a lookback price put K – S_{min}

In theory, lookback options should be quite popular. The feature of selling at the highest or buying at the lowest price sounds tempting. However, lookback options are more expensive than standard options. This dampens their popularity.

AVERAGE OPTIONS

Average options give the option buyer the right to pay or receive the average price of an asset. Average options are also called Asian options, because they originated in Asia.

There are several types of averages: geometric, harmonic, and arithmetic. In trading practice the average is usually determined by the simplest average, the arithmetic average. This average simply adds the closing day prices of the Dow and divides it buy the number of closing days.

As with lookback options, two types of average options exist:

In an average *strike* option no constant strike is set at the trade date. The strike is the average S_{ave} that the underlying price reaches during the option period.

The payoff of an average strike *call* is the difference between the Dow at option maturity T, S_T, and the average of the Dow during the option period, S_{ave}, or zero.

$$\max (S_T - S_{ave}, 0)$$

The payoff of an average strike *put* is the difference between the average of the Dow during the option period, S_{ave}, and the Dow at option maturity T, S_T, or zero.

$$\max (S_{ave} - S_T, 0)$$

The above formulas show that an average strike call holder will buy the asset at option maturity if the average price during the life of the option is lower than the price at option maturity. Naturally, the average put strike holder will sell the underlying asset if the average Dow price is higher than the Dow price at option maturity. Figure 7.10 shows the average call on the Dow being exercised, and the average put on the Dow not being exercised.

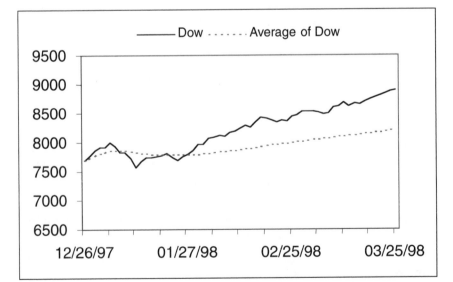

Figure 7.10   The Dow and the average of the Dow from December 26, 1997 to March 25, 1998. On March 25, 1998 the average strike call is in the money ($S_T - S_{ave} > 0$); the average strike put is out of the money ($S_{ave} - S_T < 0$).]

From Figure 7.10 we derive Method 32.

Method 32

Buy a cheap average strike put as a hedge, in order to be able to sell the Dow at its average price that occurs during the option period.

In an average *price* option a strike K is defined at the trade date, as in a standard option. At option maturity that strike and the average of the underlying price are compared.

The payoff of an average price *call* on the Dow is the difference between the average Dow price, S_{ave}, during the option period, and the strike K, or zero:

$$\max (S_{ave} - K, 0)$$

The payoff of an average price *put* on the Dow is the difference of the strike K and the average of the Dow price during the option period, S_{ave}, or zero.

$$\max (K - S_{ave}, 0)$$

In Figure 7.11, the average price put is exercised, and the average price call expires worthless.

On March 25, 1998, the average price put with a strike of 8,500 is in the money $(K - S_{ave} > 0)$; the average price call is out of the money $(S_{ave} - K < 0)$.

A big advantage of average options is that they are usually cheaper than standard options. This is because the *average* price of an asset is less volatile than the price of the asset.

In trading practice, average options are often used to protect an investment, e.g., the investment in several Dow stocks over a period of time. Therefore, an investor who wants that time period protection can employ Method 33.

Method 33

Buy a cheap average price put as a hedge to be able to achieve the difference between the strike K and the average price of the Dow that occurs during the option period.

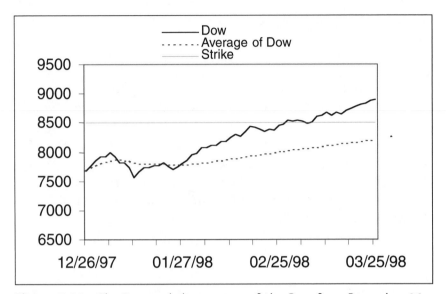

Figure 7.11   The Dow and the average of the Dow from December 26, 1997 to March 25, 1998

In practice, average options are not overly popular. However, when investors are better informed about the benefits and the low price of average options, they should become more popular in the future.

COMPOUND OPTIONS

A *compound option* is an option where the underlying instrument itself is an option. Compound options are pretty popular because they are cheap and can be used for speculation and hedging.

There are four types of compound options:

- Call on a call
- Call on a put
- Put on a call
- Put on a put

An investor can buy or sell each of these four types of compound options. If the Dow is the underlying instrument of the second option, the following holds:

- Buying a call on a call means buying the right to buy a call on the Dow. Selling a call on a call means selling the right to buy a call on the Dow.

- Buying a call on a put means buying the right to buy a put on the Dow. Selling a call on a put means selling the right to buy a put on the Dow.

- Buying a put on a call means buying the right to sell a call on the Dow. Selling a put on a call means selling the right to sell a call on the Dow.

- Buying a put on a put means buying the right to sell a put on the Dow. Selling a put on a put means selling the right to sell a put on the Dow.

(If all this sounds confusing, read it over!)

As shown in Figure 7.12, there are three important dates when pricing compound options.

Let's discuss the functioning of compound options by looking at a call on a call on the Dow.

At t_0, the premium for the 1 (compound) option is paid and the strike prices K_1 and K_2 are negotiated and set. For example, today a premium of \$0.5 is paid for the right to buy a call on the Dow at a premium \$3 (K_1). This call might have a strike of 9,500 Dow points (K_2).

At T_1, the 1 (compound) option will be exercised, if the strike K_1 of the first option is lower than the present value of the 2. (underlying) option. If the compound option was exercised at T_1, the 2. (underlying) option might be exercised at T_2. It will be exercised if the strike K_2 of the underlying option is lower than the price of the Dow S_{T_2}.

It should be mentioned that the investor owns a *standard* call with a strike of K_2 and a maturity of T_2 if he has exercised the compound option at T_1.

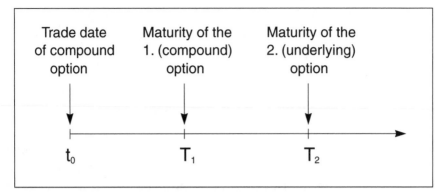

Figure 7.12   Crucial dates of a compound option

Most compound options have a higher leverage effect than standard options (see Chapter 4, Table 4.3). Therefore, in trading practice, compound options are often used to speculate.

However, compound options are usually used for hedging. This can be explained with a *cap* example. A cap is an insurance against rising interest rates.

Say an entrepreneur does not know if he will win a competitive bid for an investment project, which starts in three months. He can buy a call on a cap, called a caption. This gives the investor the right to buy the cap in three months at a price that is determined today. In three months, the entrepreneur will have the following four choices:

- If the entrepreneur wins the bidding and needs the cap and the cap has gotten more expensive (due to rising interest rates or higher implied volatility), the entrepreneur will exercise the option on the cap and buy the cap cheaply.

- If the entrepreneur wins the bidding and needs the cap, but cap prices have fallen, the entrepreneur will not exercise the caption and will buy a cap at the lower market price.

- If the entrepreneur does not win the bidding and does not need the cap, he will, if cap prices have risen, buy the cap and sell it at a profit in the market.

- If the entrepreneur does not win the bidding and cap prices have fallen, the caption will expire worthless. However, since the premiums of captions are generally low, the loss is rather small.

Using compound options as hedge, we derive Method 34.

Method 34

Buy a very cheap and highly leveraged call on a put if you are not very sure about the Dow movement, but still want to protect against a decreasing Dow.

This method will allow an investor to buy a put on the Dow at T_1 cheaply (see Figure 7.12), if the Dow has decreased from today to T_1. The investor can sell the put at T_1 at a profit. If the investor keeps the put, he is insured against a further decline of the Dow from T_1 to T_2.

Compound options can also be used to speculate, as in Method 35.

Method 35

Buy a very cheap and highly leveraged call on a call if you are not very sure about the Dow movement, but still want to participate in a rising Dow.

Method 35 will allow the investor to buy a call on the Dow cheaply at T_1 (see Figure 7.12), if the Dow has increased from today until T_1. The investor can sell the call at T_1 with a profit. If the investor keeps the call, he will participate in an increasing Dow from T_1 to T_2.

Chooser Options

*Choosers are not creations from my
heat-oppressed brain.*

—Mark Rubinstein

A popular variation of compound options are *chooser* or "as you like it" options. A chooser option is an option where at some point in time, the option buyer can determine if the option is a call or a put.

Chooser options have high customer appeal and are often issued as warrants. Warrants are standardized, securitized options for the small investor. As early as 1990, Bankers Trust issued chooser options on the German Dax and on crude oil.

Buying a chooser makes sense if the investor believes in high Dow volatility but does not know where the Dow is going. In particular, buying a chooser is sensible if after a certain event, e.g., an election or the release of a crucial economic figure, the Dow is expected to establish a new downward or upward trend. If the event initiates an upward trend, the chooser will naturally be transformed into a call; if the event establishes a downward trend, the chooser will become a put. Figure 7.13 shows how a chooser option works.

Chooser options are cheaper than their relatives, the straddles (see Chapter 5, Figures 5.5 and 5.6). This is because once the choice is made, the option buyer owns only a call *or* a put, whereas in a straddle a call *and* a put is owned. Choosers are, therefore, sometimes referred to as "discount straddles."

From Figure 7.13 we derive Method 36.

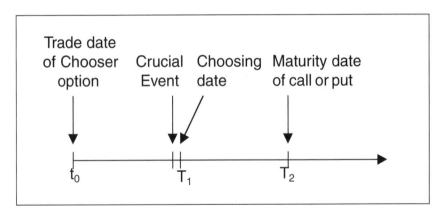

Figure 7.13   A chooser option with the choosing date closely after a crucial event that determines the future Dow direction

Method 36

Buy a cheap chooser option with a choosing date closely after an event that determines the future Dow movement.

MULTI-ASSET OR CORRELATION OPTIONS

It takes rain and sun to make a rainbow.

Multi-asset options are options whose payoff depends on the price of two or more assets. There are — to no one's surprise — a huge variety of multi-asset options, also called rainbow options, that trade in the financial markets. In practice, multi-asset options are used for speculative and hedging purposes.

The following multi-asset options are the most popular in the market.

Payoff at Option Maturity

Option on the better of two	$\max(S_1, S_2)$
Option on the worse of two	$\min(S_1, S_2)$
Option on better of two or cash	$\max(S_1, S_2, \text{Cash})$
Call on the maximum of two	$\max[0, (S_1, S_2) - K]$
Exchange option	$\max(0, S_2 - S_1)$
Spread option	$\max[0, (S_2 - S_1) - K]$
Guaranteed return on investment (Groi)	$\max(S_1 - K, \text{Premium})$
Dual strike option	$\max(0, S_1 - K_1, S_2 - K_2)$
Portfolio or basket option	$\max = \left(\sum_{i=1}^{n} n_i S_i - K, 0 \right)$

---

n_i = number of shares or weight of asset S_i

Let's look at the types of multi-asset options in detail. The buyer of an *option on the better of two* pays a premium today and has the right to receive asset 1 (e.g., 100 IBM stocks), or asset 2 (e.g., 100 Yahoo stocks) at option maturity. The option buyer will naturally choose to receive the stock with the higher price. This leads us to Method 37.

Method 37

Buy an option on the better of two if you believe that at option maturity either asset 1 or asset 2 will have a higher price than the option premium.

The buyer of an *option on the worse of two* pays a premium today and will receive the asset with the lower price at option maturity. Options on the worse of two are not very frequently traded.

The buyer of an *option on the better of two or cash* pays a premium today and at option maturity, receives asset 1, asset 2, or the agreed cash amount, whatever is highest. Thus, we derive Method 38.

Method 38

Buy an option on the better of two or cash if you believe that at option maturity either asset 1 or asset 2 will have a higher price than the option premium, but you want to secure yourself against neither of the assets increasing.

If neither of the two assets increases, the investor will at least get the previously negotiated amount of cash.

The buyer of a *call on the maximum of two* pays a premium today. At option maturity he receives the difference between the more costly stock and the strike K, if this difference is positive. Otherwise, the option expires worthless.

Method 39

Buy a call on the maximum of two if you believe that at option maturity the difference between the higher of two asset prices and a strike K will be higher than the option premium.

The buyer of an *exchange option* pays a premium today. At option maturity he receives the difference between asset 2 and asset 1, if this difference is positive. Otherwise, the option expires worthless.

Method 40

Buy an exchange option, if you believe that at option maturity the difference between asset S_2 and asset S_1 will be higher than the option premium.

The buyer of a *spread option* pays a premium today. At option maturity the option buyer receives the difference between asset 2 minus asset 1 and the strike K, if the difference is positive. Otherwise, the option expires worthless.

Method 41

Buy a spread option if you believe that at option maturity the difference between two assets compared with a strike K will be higher than the option premium.

The buyer of a *guaranteed return on investment (GROI)* will at least get back the premium that was paid at option start. If the asset price minus the strike price is higher than the premium, the buyer will receive the asset price minus the strike. GROI have been around for a while and are popular instruments. The seller makes money on the time value of the premium, i.e., the premium is worth less at option maturity than at the earlier option start.

Method 42

Buy a guaranteed return on investment (GROI) if you believe that at option maturity the underlying asset price will be higher than the strike, but you want at least your invested money back.

The buyer of a *dual strike option* pays a premium today. At option maturity he receives the higher of asset 1 minus a strike K_1 and asset 2 minus strike K_2, if one of the two are positive. Otherwise, the option expires worthless.

Method 43

Buy a dual strike option if you believe that at option maturity the difference between an asset 1 and a strike 1, or an asset 2 and strike 2 will be higher than the option premium.

The buyer of a *portfolio or basket option* pays a premium today. At option maturity he receives the highest difference between a certain asset out of a number of assets and a strike K. If none of the assets exceed the strike K, the option expires worthless.

Multi-asset options frequently occur in the credit market, especially as exchange and spread options. One of the most popular credit derivatives is the *Total Rate of Return Swap*. Here the price change plus the coupon of a risky bond (e.g., a Russian bond) is exchanged for the price change plus the coupon of a riskless bond (e.g., a U.S. treasury bond).

This Total Rate of Return swap can be priced as an exchange option. The option buyer buys the right to exchange the total return of a risky asset (S_1) for a secure asset (S_2). Figure 7.14 shows an example of a Total Rate of Return Swap. If the investor wants to relate the difference in the return of two assets to a strike K, he or she can buy a spread option to reduce the credit risk.

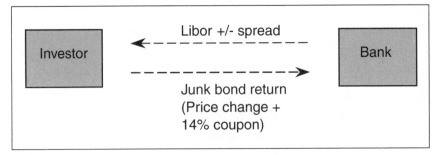

Figure 7.14 A Total Rate of Return Swap. The investor swaps his risky return into a safe Libor (London Interbank offered rate) interest rate return

Quanto Options

A further popular correlation option is the quanto option. A *Quanto option* is an option that allows a domestic investor to exchange the potential payoff in a foreign currency back into the home currency at a fixed exchange rate.

Therefore, a quanto option protects an investor against currency risk. Let's assume an American believes the Japanese Nikkei will increase, but is worried about a decreasing yen. The investor can buy a quanto call on the Nikkei, with the yen payoff being converted into dollars at a fixed (usually today's) exchange rate.

The term quanto comes from quantity, meaning that the exact amount that is re-exchanged to the home currency is unknown, because it depends on the payoff of the option. Therefore the financial institution selling a quanto call does not know two things:

1. How deep will the call on the Nikkei be in the money, thus, how much yen will be converted into dollars
2. What is the exchange rate at option maturity, at which point the stochastic yen payoff will be converted into dollars

The correlation between the two unknowns, the price of the underlying S and the exchange rate X, significantly influences the quanto option price.

If the correlation is positive, an increasing Nikkei will also mean an increasing yen. That is in the call seller's favor. The payoff must be settled, but only requires a small yen amount to achieve the dollar payment. Therefore, the more positive the correlation coefficient, the lower the price for the quanto option.

If the correlation coefficient is negative, then the opposite applies: If the Nikkei increases, the yen decreases in value. Therefore more yen are needed to meet the dollar payment. Therefore, the lower the correlation coefficient, the more expensive the quanto option.

Method 44

Buy a Quanto call option on a foreign asset if you believe that the asset will increase and you want to protect yourself against currency risk.

COMBINATIONS OF EXOTIC OPTIONS

---

*Die Gedanken sind frei
(There are no limits to human fantasy).*

Combinations of all exotic options discussed so far in this chapter are possible and trade in the financial market. One of the most popular combinations are convertibles. A *convertible,* in its simplest form, is a bond that can be converted into a pre-defined number of stocks.

Therefore, the downside risk of a convertible is limited because the bond will redeem at par, *and* a convertible has the upside potential of a stock.

To explain a convertible, let's assume that in a convertible, one bond with a principal of $100 can be converted into 4 shares. If at maturity of the convertible, the stock's price is $30, conversion is sensible, because the conversion value $4 \times \$30 = \$120$ is higher than the bond value of $100.

During the life of the convertible, the conversion value is higher than at maturity, because of the time value of a convertible. Convertibles can usually be converted into a stock at any time during the life of the convertible, thus they are American style.

During the life of the convertible, it has the feature of an exchange option (discussed previously): A bond can be exchanged for a stock. S_1 is the price of the bond, S_2 is the price of the stock (times the number of stocks that may be converted).

However, there are some additional features that a make a convertible more troublesome to value:

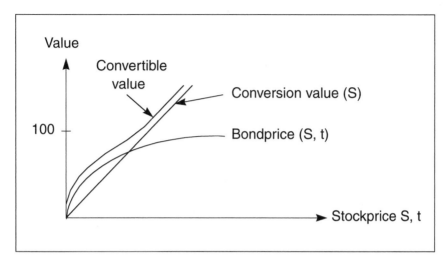

Figure 7.15 Conversion value and bond price as the lower boundaries for the value of a convertible

- A convertible is usually issued below par, because the coupon of a convertible is lower than the market coupon. Thus, the price of a convertible bond increases to par when approaching the maturity of the bond. Therefore, the strike of the exchange option S_1 (being identical with the price of the bond) increases steadily as time passes.

- In practice, convertibles are usually Bermuda style barrier callable. This means that the issuer can buy back the convertible at predefined dates at par, if the bond price reaches certain barriers. Naturally, this feature complicates the pricing of a convertible significantly. Now not only the convertible holder has an option, but also the convertible issuer! However in practice, convertible issuers sometimes do not call the convertible, although it is sensible from a financial point of view. The reason is that convertibles are sometimes issued as "sweeteners," as a public relations tool to improve customer relations. This makes convertibles more valuable than the numerical valuation procedure implies.

- Additionally, some convertibles have a put option that the convertible buyer holds on the convertible.

All this makes convertibles pretty difficult to price. One thing we know for sure is that the maximum of the bond price and the conversion value serve as lower boundaries for the value of convertibles (see Figure 7.15).

All this leads us to our final method, Method 45.

Method 45

Buy a convertible on a stock if you believe the stock price will rise and you want your investment to at least redeem at the par value of the bond.

SUMMARY

This final chapter explained the most popular exotic options and derived methods to achieve high returns using exotic options.

Exotic options are options whose payoff, valuation, and hedging procedures are different and usually more complicated than those of standard options. Exotic options have become increasingly popular in the recent past. The reason is that many exotics can precisely replicate an investor's view about market movements. The main reason for the use of exotic options in the financial markets is speculation. Some exotics, however, are utilized for hedging purposes such as quantos and average options.

The standard exotic options can be categorized into seven groups.

- Digital options
- Barrier options
- Lookback options
- Average options
- Compound options
- Multi-asset or correlation options
- Hybrids

Cash or nothing digital options, also called bet options, have a payoff of zero or a fixed amount of cash. Though not too popular, they serve as a basis to construct more complex exotic options, such as the contingent premium option. A contingent premium option is an option where the option buyer pays the option premium at option maturity, only if the option finishes in the money. At the money contingent premium options are about twice as expensive as the equivalent standard options, which reduces their popularity.

Barrier options are one of the most popular types of exotic options, especially in the currency market. The major types of barrier options trade on the CBOE (Chicago Board of Options Exchange). There are two types of barrier options: Knock-in options and knock-out options. Both types are cheaper than the equivalent standard options, which is one reason for the popularity of barriers. Also, barrier options can precisely reflect an investor's view of the underlying asset. Knock-out barrier options are sometimes used as a hedge. This is quite risky. The option might get knocked out, so the investor becomes un-hedged.

Lookback options allow the buyer to buy the Dow at the lowest level or sell it at the highest level that the Dow reaches during the option period. In a lookback strike option, the maximum or minimum of the Dow during the option period is compared with the Dow at maturity. In a lookback price option the maximum or minimum of the Dow during the option period is compared with an exogenous strike. Lookback options are quite popular. Naturally, they are more expensive than standard options, which dampens their customer appeal.

Average options give the option buyer the right to pay or receive the average price of an asset. As with lookback options, average strike and average price options exist. Average options are usually cheaper than standard options, because the average of the security is less volatile than the security itself. Average options are usually used to hedge, e.g., if the investor wants to protect an investment over a certain period of time. Average options will be become more popular in the future, when investors are better informed about the benefits and better pricing and hedging methods are found.

A compound option is an option where the underlying instrument itself is an option. There are four basic types of compounds. Calls on calls, calls on puts, puts on calls, and puts on puts. Compound options are very cheap and offer high leverage. Therefore they are popular instruments, especially if an investor is quite uncertain about the market, but still wants to participate in an upward or downward move. A popular type of compound option is the chooser option. In a chooser option, the buyer can decide at a certain point of time if the option is a call or a put. Chooser warrants (options for the small investor) often trade on exchanges.

Multi-asset options, also called correlation options, are options whose payoff depends on the price of two or more assets. There are many types of multi-asset options, the most popular being the exchange option, spread option, and the guaranteed return on investment (Groi). A special type of correlation option is the quanto option. Here an investor can invest in a foreign asset without currency risk.

Combinations of all the above-mentioned exotic options exist. One of the most popular combinations are convertibles, which are often issued as double exchange options. Thus, the convertible holder has the option to convert a bond into a stock, however, the convertible issuer has the option to buy back the bond at certain dates at par. More exotic options and combinations are likely to occur in the future to satisfy exotic innovation fetishism.

SUGGESTED READING

Bergman, Y., "Pricing Path Contingent Claims," *Research in Finance* 5, pp. 229–241.

Boyle, P., J. Evnine, and S. Gibbs, (1989). "Numerical Evaluation of Multivariate Contingent Claims," *Review of Financial Studies,* 2(2), pp. 241–50.

Boyle, P., and S. H. Lau, (1994). "Bumping Up Against the Barrier with the Binomial Method," *Journal of Derivatives, 1*(4), pp. 6–14.

Brennan, M. J., and E. S. Schwartz, (1982). "An Equilibrium Model of Bond Pricing and a Test of Market Efficiency," *Journal of Financial and Quantitative Analysis,* 17(3), pp. 301–29.

Cox, J., Ingersoll, J., Ross, S., (1985). "A Theory of Term Structure of Interest Rates," *Econometrica,* pp. 385–407.

Drezner, Z., (1978). "Computation of the Bivariate Normal Integral," *Mathematics of Computation,* pp. 277–299.

Duffie, D., (1992). *Dynamic Asset Pricing Theory,* (Princeton, NJ: Princeton University Press).

Duffie, D., and K. J. Singleton, (1994). "Econometric Modeling of Term Structure of Defaultable Bonds," (Stanford, CA: Stanford University).

Garman, M., (1989). "Recollection in Tranquility," *RISK,* March.

Geske, R., (1979). "The Valuation of Compound Options," *Journal of Financial Economics,* 7, pp. 63–81.

Goldman, B., H. Sosin, and A. Gatto, (1979). "Path Dependent Options: Buy at the Low, Sell at the high," *Journal of* Finance, 34, pp. 1111–1127.

Hauswald, R., (1992). "Martingaltheorien und Finanzthoery: Ein Ueberblick", Stanford University Paper.

Heath, D., A. Jarrow, and A. Morton, (1990). "Bond Pricing and the Term Structure of Interest Rates: A Discrete Time Approximation," *Journal of Financial and Quantitative Analysis,* 25(4), pp. 419–40.

Heath, D., R. Jarrow, A. Morton, and M. Spindel, (1993). "Easier Done Than Said," *RISK,* May, pp. 77–80.

Heyen, R., and H. Kat, (1996). "Crossing Barriers," *RISK,* June, pp. 46–51.

Ho, T. S. Y., and S.-B. Lee, (1986). "Term Structure Movements and Pricing Interest Rate Contingent Claims," *Journal of Finance,* 41, pp. 1011–29.

Hudson, M., (1991). "The Value of Going Out," *RISK,* March.

Hull, J. C., (1997). *Options, Futures, and Other Derivatives,* Third ed., (Upper Saddle River, NJ: Prentice Hall).

Hull, J. C., and A. White, (1993). "Finding the Keys," *RISK,* September.

Hull, J. C., and A. White, (1992). "Root and Branch," *RISK,* December, pp. 101–6.

Jamshidian, F., (1994). "Corralling Quantos," *RISK,* March.

Jarrow, R. A., (1995). *Modeling Fixed Income Securities and Interest Rate Options,* (New York: McGraw-Hill).

Kemna, A., A. Vorst, (1990). "A Pricing Method for Options Based on Average Asset Values." *Journal of Banking and Finance,* pp. 113–129.

Margrave, W., "The Valuation of an Option to Exchange One Asset for Another," *Journal of Finance,* 33, pp. 177–186.

Nelken, I., (1993). "Square Deals" *RISK,* pp. 56–59.

Reiner, E., (1992). "Quanto Mechanics," *RISK,* March, pp. 147–154.

Rubinstein, M., (1991). "Breaking Down the Barriers," *RISK,* September.

Rubinstein, M., (1992). "Double Trouble," *RISK,* January.

Rubinstein, M., (1991). "One for Another," *RISK*, pp. 191–194.

Rubinstein, M., (1991). "Pay Now Chose Later," *RISK*, February.

Rubinstein, M., (1991). "Somewhere Over the Rainbow," *RISK*, November.

Rubinstein, M., (1991). "Two in One," *RISK*, May.

Schaefer, S., E. Schwarz, "Time Dependent Variance and the Pricing of Bond Options," *Journal of Finance* 42, 1113–1128.

Smithson, C., (1992). "Wonderful Life," *RISK*, pp. 23–32.

Steen, N., G. Byrne, and E. Gelbard, (1969). "Gaussian Quadratures for the Integral," *Mathematics of Computation,* 23, pp. 661–671.

Stulz, R., (1982). "Options on the Minimum or Maximum of Two Assets," *Journal of Financial Economics,* 10, pp. 161–85.

INDEX